THE DYNAMIC POWER OF

SOUTHERN SHAOLIN KUNG FU

RONALD WHEELER

BEGINNER TO INTERMEDIATE
JOW GA KUNG FU

Ron's Martial Fitness
www.ronsmartialfitness.com

THE DYNAMIC POWER OF
SOUTHERN SHAOLIN KUNG FU

RONALD WHEELER
BEGINNER TO INTERMEDIATE
JOW GA KUNG FU

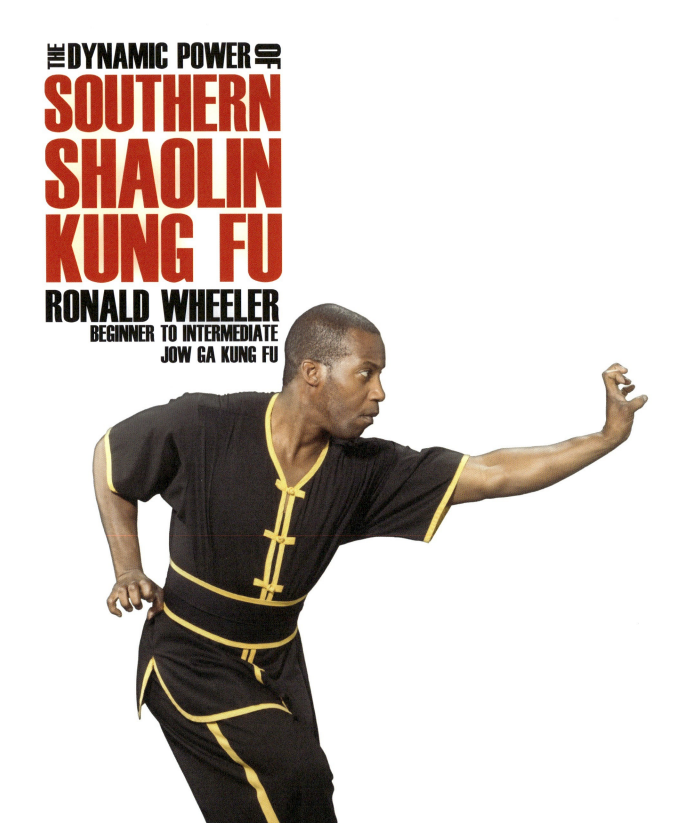

Acknowledgments

To the late Grand Master Chan Man Cheung (1929-2013), thank you for helping spread the Jow Ga system to the United States.

To the late Jow Ga Master Dean Chin (1947-1985) the father of American Jow Ga Kung Fu, your memory lives on in all of those you've inspired and taught.

To my parents, the late Mr. and Mrs. Clarence Wheeler, thank you for allowing me to pursue my dream in martial arts.

To my photographer, Moshe Zusman of Moshe Zusman Photography Studio (www.moshezusman.com), with your talent and expertise, you have helped the world see the Jow Ga system more brilliantly.

To Jessic Mitchell, Jr. (Martial Artist and MMA Fighter), thank you for assisting me in the making of this work.

To my designer and multimedia specialist, Sandra Cantrell, thank you for bringing all the elements of this work together.

TABLE OF CONTENTS

Introduction

Shaolin martial arts has a rich and vibrant history that spans over 1500 years. Over 100 well known Shaolin martial arts systems claim to trace their roots back to either the Northern or Southern Shaolin temples of China. The system originally known as Hung Tao Choy Mei is among these 100 timeless styles. Yet, this unique system bares the distinction of having has its roots firmly planted in both Shaolin temples. By embracing styles and techniques of northern and southern martial arts, this system possesses a balanced blend of its homeland. This particular system was later renamed Jow Ga Kung Fu in honor of its principal founder, Jow Lung. Since its creation, Jow Ga has become one of the fastest growing styles of Kung Fu worldwide. Jow Ga practitioners can be found on all continents with thriving schools in the United States, Poland, Brazil, Germany, England, Italy, and of course various Asian countries. However, here within the United States, the Dean Chin branch of the Jow Ga system is recognized as the oldest version of Jow Ga having been founded in the Nation's Capitol in the China town section of Washington, D.C. in 1968. As well, the Dean Chin branch is the most well known within the United States. This book will take the reader from the beginner to the intermediate levels of the Dean Chin branch of Jow Ga. It will also introduce the reader to two well known forms within the system that were created during the life of Jow Lung. These two forms, "Big Controlling Tiger Fist" and "Plum Blossom Spear", have never been revealed to students outside of the system until the publication of this work. It is my sincere wish that the reader of this work gains a better understanding of the boxing skills within the Jow Ga system as well as an insight into the martial arts as a whole.

– **Ronald Wheeler**

Foreword
from Kenny Chin

Jow Ga Master Dean Chin was the son of my elder uncle. He and I grew up together on the Kowloon side of Hong Kong and actually lived in the very same apartment building just two floors away from each other. As we were growing up, I always remembered him as a very trustworthy and respectable young man. It was Dean Chin himself who inspired me to get involved in the martial arts which I continue to practice to this day.

His devotion and commitment to the martial arts and in particular the Jow Ga system gained him much respect from his Master Chan Man Cheung. It is my opinion that Master Cheung cared deeply for my cousin and thus spent many hours fine tuning his kung fu skill. I was filled with great sadness and shock at the untimely passing of my cousin in 1985 who I will always remember as being very good to me. To lose a man of his skill and talent at such a young age is hard to even imagine.

As the years passed I had no idea of what had become of my cousin's school or the system he championed. Then, I had the great fortune of meeting Ron Wheeler, a young student of my cousin. I read his work, "The Power Of Shaolin Kung Fu", which is to my knowledge the first book written on the Jow Ga system outside of Asia. Then, having an opportunity to actually meet with Ron and see his skill first hand made me very happy and gave me the chance to see my cousin again in spirit.

In the almost 30 years since the passing of Master Dean Chin, I have not met anyone from my cousin's school with as much dedication and drive to promote not only the Jow Ga system, but my cousin as well. Ron's commitment to Jow Ga reminds me so much of his teachers. Not only has he been a tournament champion many times over, he has made the system available to many who would otherwise not have the chance to experience one of the great treasures of China. Ron also continues to keeping my cousin's vision alive by having the first accredited class on the Jow Ga system of kung fu at George Washington University in our nation's capitol of Washington, D.C.

I am truly honored to know Sifu Ron Wheeler. I trust him to continue to bring honor and respect to the art of Chinese kung fu and to his late Master, my cousin Chin Yuk Din (Dean Chin).

PHOTOGRAPH BY MICHELLE ROBINSON

– Choy Li Fut Master Kenny Chin
Chin Kwok Chee
1st Cousin of Dean Chin

Vincent Lyn Remembers

I first met Sifu Ron Wheeler at a Chinese martial arts tournament held at Murry Bergtraum High School in Chinatown, NYC. I had a number of students competing that day and one of my senior instructors seemed to get stuck competing against Sifu Wheeler in every single event he was in. Whether that was a bad omen for my student that remains to be seen. Nonetheless, it certainly was a learning experience of a force to be reckoned with. I remember saying to Ron, "Is there anything you're not competing in so at least my instructor has a chance to maybe place 2nd or 3rd?" If my memory serves me correctly, Ron competed in 7 or 8 different events that day running from one to another from empty hands to short weapons to long weapons with hardly a break to compose himself and yet he seemed with vicarious ease to win everything. I applauded him, though, at the same time stamping my feet in sheer frustration. My student competed in Southern empty hands form and we decided to do Ling Gar and it was a flawless showing. Ron even came up to me and said, "Wow, I really like that form and would love to learn it." Yet, as flawless as it was he (Ron) won yet again. Sifu Ron Wheeler is a consummate martial artist, an incredible competitor, but an extremely humble and honorable human being. I have great respect for his knowledge of martial arts history & culture and his true martial spirit. We recently met again after many years in NYC, Chinatown and sat down with other Sifus for the traditional Dim Sum brunch. It was wonderful seeing him again after over 15 years passing and he hadn't aged a day. More humble and astute than ever, truly gracious, and respectful. Without a moment's hesitation he poured tea for everyone and as my cup became empty it was full again. Sifu Ron Wheeler, you are a true gentleman. I take my hat off to you. Peace.

PHOTOGRAPH BY BOB CAPAZZO

– Master Vincent Lyn
Model, Concert Pianist, Actor
Co-star with Jackie Chan in *Operation Condor*

Brief History of the Jow Ga System

The Jow Ga system started off in a very unique way. First of all this particular style of kung fu has not one, but five founders which are known as Ng Fu Jow or the Five Tigers of the Jow family. They are Jow Lung the oldest of the five son's, Jow Hip, followed by the twin boys Jow Biu and Jow Hoy and finally the youngest brother Jow Tin who was the last of the Five Tigers to pass away in 1972.

Jow Lung who is considered the main founder of the system first combined techniques from both the Hung Ga and Choy Ga systems into a new style which was he named Hung Tao Choy Mei (Head of Hung, Feet of Choy). This phrase loosely translated means that from the waste up the hand techniques performed comes from the Hung Ga system, and from the waste down the foot work patterns comes from the Choy Ga system. So in the beginning, the system was very much a purely southern style. It wasn't until Jow Lung made a trip to Malaysia that the northern side of the system came in to play.

Because of the economic hardships of the time, Jow Lung traveled to Malaysia to try and find work, but by a strange twist of fate found himself in a monastery learning a version of Northern Shaolin kung fu from the abbot of the temple named Chian Yi. After nearly five years of temple life, Jow Lung decided to return home. Before he left, however, the abbot suggested to him that he combine all that he knew into a new and more complete system utilizing the best techniques of both southern and northern styles of Shaolin Kung fu.

Shortly after his return home, Jow Lung learned of a contest being given by a Warlord General named Lee Fook Lam in order to find a skilled teacher to train his troops. Over 100 potential teachers competed in the event. After many days of fighting, Jow Lung armed with his new creation stood victorious and the style that would go on to be known as Jow Ga kung fu would become famous along with its creator.

However, this momentous occasion would be short lived. Jow Lung the creator of the style that would bear his family name, passed away at the age of 29 as a result of pneumonia. With his passing, the remaining brothers selected Jow Biu to spear-head and oversee the growth of the system. Jow Biu made the system of his family a force to be reckoned with from the very beginning. His talent knew no bounds with the creation of many sets that are still taught to this day. The form known as Fa Keun (Flower Fist) was created by Jow Biu when he gave an impromptu performance at a banquet in Hong Kong.

While on a trip to Hong Kong in July of 2009, I discovered that upon his appointment to promote and lead the system of his family, Jow Biu was challenged by other martial artist nearly every day for about two years. It was said that he never lost a match. The thing most remarkable about this is that he was only 20 years of age at this time and stood only about 5'3" in height.

It was also told to me that by the time he arrived in Hong Kong in the 1950's that no one dared challenge him as his reputation as a fighter had spread far and wide. During his life as a martial artist, Jow Biu was respected by many in the kung fu world; even those who were more senior to him.

The great Hung Ga Master Wong Fei Hung even had respect for the more junior Jow Biu as he helped Master Wong clear up a dispute between himself and a local strong man by the name of Ching Hua. Because of his fairness in handling the matter, Mok Gwai Lan who was the wife of Wong Fei Hung wanted to adopt Jow Biu into the Wong family.

Jow Biu's life was truly great as he taught many the art of this family. One of these students, Grand Master Chan Man Cheung, would go on to bring even greater fame to the Jow Ga system as he would be known not only as a skilled fighter, but also as "The Lion King" because of his expertise in the art of Lion Dancing.

His skill in Lion Dancing was so great that he was asked to perform the welcoming Lion Dance for a young Queen Elizabeth when Hong Kong was still under the rule of Great Britain. I can remember meeting Grand Master Chan for the first time in 1988 and having him show me and my training brothers and sisters many new maneuvers they were doing with the Lion back in Hong Kong. I tell you no lie, he killed us! I've never seen a man with so much energy. There I was 23 at the time, sweating bullets as he was going from one maneuver to the next without stopping to take a break, and this all after we just had dinner earlier that evening.

Until his recent passing in October of 2013, Chan Man Cheung worked tirelessly to promote and represent the system of his own Master. I once asked Grand Master Chan if he had ever learned anything else, he replied that Jow Ga had everything anyone would ever need or want in a system of martial arts. He said that all you had to do was find it through steady and diligent training. To his credit, Grand Master Chan had taught many young men the art made famous by the Five Tigers of the Jow family, but one of his students would not only become his most famous student outside of Asia, but would also go on to become known as the Father of Jow Ga kung fu in America; Dean Chin.

Master Chin Yuk Din (Dean Chin) was a pioneer in terms of martial arts here in America as he was the first to teach traditional kung fu south of New York City in 1968. He was also the first to teach Non-Asians in the Washington, D.C. metropolitan area the true art of Chinese kung fu. Before that, it was only taught to those of Chinese ancestry.

Master Chin was also the first teacher at that time to teach aspects of other Chinese systems to his students. In effect, Master Chin was ahead of his time here in the nation's capitol as he basically had his students cross training in order to give them a better understanding of Chinese martial arts. Because Master Chin knew so much, it was not uncommon for him to teach his more senior students forms and techniques from other well known styles such as Bak Mei (White Eyebrow) or Chut Sing Tong Long (7 Star Praying Mantis). Even village Hung Ga sets were taught to those he felt were deserving of this knowledge.

In 1979, Master Chin was selected to compete in the World Kuoshu Championship held in Taipei, Taiwan. His team which won top honors and was honored with a write up in the *Washington Post* newspaper was comprised completely of African Americans. This very unique fact is just one of the things that set Master Chin apart as he would tell his students many times over, " You can be as good as anyone Chinese. All you have to do is practice."

Master Chin however, would not live long enough to see his school and the system he brought to America flourish into what it is today. In August of 1985, Master Dean Chin passed away at the young age of 35. His death so stunned the martial arts community that many thought the school he built and the system he promoted would surely fall to dust. However, thanks to the dedication and hard work of many of Master Chin's students, the Jow Ga system has grown well beyond the confines of D.C.'s China Town. Within the D.C. metropolitan area, which includes the states of Maryland and Virginia, the Jow Ga system has grown from one to nearly fourteen schools.

The system has even reached levels of higher learning as there is now a Jow Ga class being taught at George Washington University. This is the first traditional kung fu class being taught for credit at a major university. With schools in countries such as Basil, Poland, England, and of course Mainland China as well as the United States, the Jow Ga system has quickly become one of the fastest growing styles of kung fu in the world.

Chapter One:
Stepping Form

STEPPING FORM

Within traditional and contemporary Chinese martial arts a strong and solid foundation is needed in order to attain a high level of skill in one's chosen style. One of the oldest and best ways to achieve this is by way of stance training. This can be done in two ways; static or active training.

Static training involves sitting in one or more of the various stances your style may teach for an extended period of time. For example, one could sit in the Four Level Horse stances starting off for two to three minutes at a time and extending the time to ten minutes or longer. I can remember that in the school of Master Dean Chin, anytime you were late for class, whoever was teaching would have you sit in your horse stance in the corner of the class room until they allowed you to participate.

Active training involves using many if not all of the various stances taught within your system in an exercise designed to not only strengthen your legs but teach you how to move toward and away from your opponent employing various offensive and defensive techniques to your advantage. Choy Li Fut's 5 Wheel stance exercise is probably the most well known of all the formal stance drills taught within kung fu circles.

In the Dean Chin branch of the Jow Ga system the exercise known simply as the Stepping Form was created some time in the early 1970's. It's intended purpose was to not only strengthen the legs of the potential student but to teach proper footwork needed for the execution of all techniques taught within the Jow Ga system.

Most Southern long range styles of kung fu use what is known as Ten Pattern Stepping or Sup Jee Bo footwork. This means that the footwork found in these styles of kung fu resemble the Chinese character for the number Ten which looks like the Plus sign for arithmetic's in America and most nations around the world. Therefore the footwork for these particular styles of kung fu follows the directions of North, South, West and East.

The Jow Ga system, however, is famous for its Eight Trigram Stepping or Ba Qua Bo style of footwork which not only covers the directions of North, South, West and East, it also covers the other four directions of North/East, South/East, North/West and South/West giving the student greater ability to attack and defend from any and all directions.

The Stepping Form as I learned it during the time of Master Chin's life was less than 40 movements in length. However, it has been expanded to about double that length to include such maneuvers as the Iron Broom technique which is a low sweeping leg maneuver designed to up-end an opponent.

Another technique added to the Stepping Form is the maneuver Mon Fu Han San (Tiger Running Down the Mountain). Mon Fu Han San is a footwork series which uses the Cross Stance in conjunction with the Butterfly Hand technique (Woo Dip Sao). It is designed to first retreat from then quickly close the distance on an opponent knocking them down with a Double Palm strike or a simultaneous Palm strike and Reverse Sweep combination to the back of the opponent's leg.

The Stepping Form taught within this text will be referred to as the First Generation form as it was created at the time of Master Chin's life and was taught to all of his students until the time of his passing. However, this does not in any way diminish or suggest that students who learned this set after Master Chin's death are not from the Dean Chin lineage, only that they learned it after other Senior students of Dean Chin made what I would call dramatic improvements within the form thereby giving the Jow Ga student greater versatility in the usage of their footwork and the application of their techniques.

1. Start from the ready position.

2. Open to the Sei Ping Ma.

3. Shuffle 3 times to the Right while remaining in the Sei Ping Ma.

4. Shuffle 3 times to the Left while still in Sei Ping Ma.

5. Move forward into a Right Gung Jeen Bo then into a Left Gung Jeen Bo.

6. Step backwards into a Right Gung Jeen Bo then again into a Left Gung Jeen Bo.

7. Shuffle forward 3 times while in the Left Gung Jeen Bo.

SIDE VIEW

8. Shuffle backwards 3 times while still in a Left Gung Jeen Bo.

9. Hop in place into a Right Diu Ma.

10. Hop a second time into a Left Diu Ma.

11. Hop a third time into a Right Diu Ma.

12. Twist in place to the Right into a Right Nau Ma.

13. Snap out a Left Toe Kick stepping down into a Left Diu Ma.

14. Twist to the Left into a Left Nau Ma.

15. Snap out a Right Toe Kick stepping down into a Right Diu Ma.

16. Rotate 180 degrees to your Left into a Left Nau Ma.

17. Snap out another Right Toe Kick stepping down into a Right Diu Ma.

18. Twist again to the Right into a Right Nau Ma.

19. Snap out a Left Toe Kick and step down into the Sei Ping Ma.

20. Take the Left foot and step over the Right into a Left Nau Ma.

21. Move the Right foot and step into the Sei Ping Ma position.

22. Take the Right foot and step over the Left into a Right Nau Ma.

23. Spin 90 degrees to the Left into the Sei Ping Ma position.

24. Take a Half Step with your Right foot into a Left Gung Jeen Bo.

25. Slide the Right foot up into the Sei Ping Ma position.

26. Stand up into the Ready position and the form is complete.

Chapter Two: Ng Fu Lin Faht
Five Tiger Linking Method

2

FIVE TIGER LINKING METHOD

There is an old saying, "Only one tiger can live on top of the mountain." The tiger is the largest of the big cats in China as lions, which are larger and well known for their hunting skills, are not native to that part of the world. Tigers are known for their strong and aggressive nature in hunting and killing their prey making them the ideal inspiration for martial artist not only in China but all over the world.

Fighters who are known to be aggressive in attitude and technique and show no fear of their opponents are often referred to as tigers. On the flip side of the coin, fighters who are known more for talking a good game but not for their fighting skill are referred to as paper tigers meaning that they are all show and no go and should not be feared by their opponents in any way.

The tigers influence can be seen in many famous styles of kung fu that are based on the movements, spirit, and aggressive nature of the animal. Styles such as the Bak Fu Pai (White Tiger System), Fu Jow Pai (Tiger Claw System), and Shandong Hark Fu Jow (Shandong Black Tiger) all take their inspiration and technique from this powerful and magnificent creature.

Other famous styles of kung fu rely heavily on the use of tiger style techniques such as Bak Mei Pai (White Eyebrow System), and the Hung Fut Pai (Hung Buddha System). Even the five main southern family styles of Hung Ga, Choy Ga, Li Ga, Lau Ga, and Mok Ga are all heavily influenced by the tiger in both their technique and spirit. There are even certain techniques that cross over between southern and northern styles of kung fu that pay their respects to this beautiful animal.

One example of this crossover is the execution of a reverse punch from a bow and arrow stance. Many styles would refer to this maneuver as Black Tiger Steals the Heart. The name alone suggests to the potential student just how powerful this technique truly is and the amount of force that is to be delivered in the execution of this strike. When striking your opponent with this technique, you will in essence take away their heart, thereby taking away their will and desire to fight.

The Jow Ga system of kung fu like many other southern styles relies heavily on the use of tiger claw skills. The first form taught within the system, Siu Fok Fu Kuen or Small Subduing Tiger Fist, should tell you just how important the tiger is when it comes to combat. Although there are only a few actual tiger claw maneuvers in the form as the form itself is all about the aggressive nature of a young tiger cub.

Having practiced Jow Ga for as long as I have, there are certain techniques that I like over others. I love Tiger claw strikes! Don't blame me; blame my love of Shaw brother's films such as *Executioner of Shaolin*, or *Fist of the White Lotus*. When I saw these maneuvers on the big screen I saw not only the beauty of the technique but also their effectiveness in combat. As I got further into my training and began teaching I began looking more into these types of fighting maneuvers. Because of this, I decided to put together an exercise that would feature some of the most essential tiger claw techniques practiced within the Jow Ga system.

The Five Tiger Linking Method should be performed at full speed and power with the forcefulness of a tiger. Like all tiger claw techniques, the power comes from the legs as your stance should be solid and firm. As you start to extend the claw outward, the power is then transferred up the legs through the back and then out to the hands. When practicing this exercise, be sure to open and close the hand forcefully in order to develop strength in the muscles, joints, and tendons within the hand.

Again, balance in the execution of technique is vitally important as the exercise is performed equally on both the left and right sides of the body. A forceful vocal execution of yelling should accompany all double tiger claw techniques. The sound "Wah" should be loud and clear when striking with the tiger claw as it will add power to your strike and will also help to energize your martial spirit.

1. Stand in the Ready position.

2. Step forward into a Left Gung Jeen Bo and execute a Right Cern Fu Jow.

3. Step 45 degrees to the Right into a Right Gung Jeen Bo and strike with a Left Black Tiger Claw.

4. Step 45 degrees to the Left into a Left Gung Jeen Bo and strike with a Right Black Tiger Claw.

5. Move into a Right Nau Ma and block with a Left Fu Jeung.

6. Continue stepping around into a Left Nau Ma and block with a Right Fu Jeung.

NOTE: When putting movements 5 and 6 together the maneuver is called Tiger Brushes his Whiskers.

7. Continue moving into a Right Gung Jeen Bo and perform a Left Cern Fu Jow.

8. Move 45 degrees to the left into a Left Gung Jeen Bo and execute a Right Black Tiger Claw.

9. Step 45 degrees to the right into a Right Gung Jeen Bo and perform a Left Black Tiger Claw.

10. Take your right foot and step over your left into a Right Tau Ma while simultaneously executing a Cern Fu Jeung Strike to the groin. Left hand strikes to the Left, Right hand strikes to the Right.

11. Stand up and swing the left leg around into a Left Nau Ma grabbing with a Right Darn Fu Jow.

12. Step forward into a Right Diu Ma and strike with a Left Darn Fu Jow.

FRONT VIEW   FRONT VIEW   FRONT VIEW

13. Perform maneuvers 10 up to 12 in the opposite direction.

FRONT VIEW

14. Step over into a Left Tau Ma while performing the first section of the Woo Dip Sao. (Left hand should be in the Pak Sao position, Right hand in a low Hok Yik position.)

15. Step around into a Left Nau Ma raising both hands up and above the head.

16. Move into a Right Sei Ping Ma placing both hands on the left side of the body.

17. Shift into a Right Gung Jeen Bo and strike with the Woo Dip Fu Jow.

18. Repeat movements 14 through 17 in the opposite direction.

19. Shift into a Left Sei Ping Ma and execute a Cern Ping Jong.

20. Open up both arms into a Cern Hok Yik position.

21. Remain in the Sei Ping Ma position and perform a Right Half step while simultaneously executing a Left Pak Sao.

22. Shift back into a Right Diu Ma and perform one salute to the center.

23. Remain in the Diu Ma position extending both hands forward to a Cern Ping Choi.

24. Pull both hands back to the shoulder rolling them over to a Cern Kwa Choi.

25. Take two steps back into the ready position.

APPLICATIONS
FIRST TECHNIQUE

1. Face each other in the On Guard position.

2. Your opponent executes a Right Ping Choi.

3. Block your opponent's punch with the first half of the Cern Fu Jow sweeping the punch outward away from the body.

4. Finish the sequence by attacking the head of your opponent with the second half of the Cern Fu Jow.

Second Technique

1. Face each other in the On Guard position.

2. Your opponent executes a Right Ping Choi.

3. Twist in place into a Left Nau Ma and grab your opponent with a Right Darn Fu Jow.

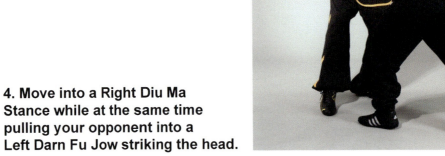

4. Move into a Right Diu Ma Stance while at the same time pulling your opponent into a Left Darn Fu Jow striking the head.

Third Technique

1. Face each other in the On Guard position.

2. Your opponent throws a high Right Round House Kick.

3. Move forward quickly into a Right Nau Ma Stance ducking under your opponent's kick.

4. After moving into position underneath your opponent attack with a Right Fu Jeung Strike to the groin. (This is known as Monkey Steals the Peach.)

Chapter Three: Fu Jow Chi Gung
Tiger Claw Chi Gung

Tiger Claw Chi Gung

Nearly all systems of Chinese martial arts whether northern or southern, external or internal believe that chi is vital to the development of the practitioner. This is done through a series of breathing exercises known as Chi Gung. Chi Gung practice varies from system to system. Some exercises may have a practitioner standing still in a very natural posture with their legs shoulder width apart and hands raised at shoulder height with both palms facing each other such as the Standing Post meditation performed by many internal styles such as Tai Chi Chuan or Ba Qua Chang.

Other styles may have the student moving from one stance to another using isotonic exercises, coordinating the movement of their hands with their breathing such as Hung Ga's famous Tit Sin Kuen (Iron Wire Fist). This particular set is so demanding on the body that I can remember one of my younger training brothers attempting to mimic the movements of this form after seeing it performed during a kung fu demo and managed to injure himself internally. I warned him not to fool around with this set, but after practicing this form incorrectly for about two days he began complaining about his right side hurting. I told him that he may have put a strain on one of his major organs; most likely his liver and that he should stop practicing this set.

As a student advances through the Jow Ga system, one will notice that many of the forms such as Dai Fok Fu Kuen (Big Subduing Tiger Fist) or Fu Pow Kuen (Tiger Cougar Fist) have a generous amount of isotonic movement built into them through which chi is developed. When talking to the head of the Jow Biu Association in Hong Kong, China who was as well a second generation practitioner of Jow Ga, it was confirmed that when one first starts to learn the Big Tiger set, the practitioner will tire easily. Yet, after constant and diligent practice the student will gain tremendous power and their health will greatly improve.

Through years of practice and study with various masters of both Northern and Southern styles of kung fu, I decided to put together a Chi Gung exercise with a two fold purpose. The first was to give the potential Jow Ga student more power in the delivery of their techniques. Second was to improve the overall health of the student by introducing them to the concept of chi at an earlier stage in their training so that by the time they began learning sets such as Big Subduing Tiger they could perform them without tiring.

This exercise called Fu Jow Gung (Tiger Claw Chi Gung) is a relatively short set containing only 40 plus movements. However, when practiced regularly and properly the practitioner will notice their energy and power are greatly increased.

There are two important points I would like to stress when practicing this or any type of Chi Gung exercise. The first is that proper alignment of the body with the spine and head straight in conjunction with proper breathing is essential to the development of chi flow. The second point to stress is that one should never practice this type of Chi Gung exercise too soon before going to bed as you will have a great deal of trouble sleeping due to the fact that your body is now charged and full of energy.

1. Open to the Sei Ping Ma position.

2. Execute a Biu Jee Strike downward at 45 degrees with the Right hand.

3. Bring the Right hand up to the Mei Yun Jiu Geang position.

5. Using Isotonic movement push the palm forwards as if you where pushing against a wall and having it move slowly away from you.

4. Move the Right hand across the chest from left to right with the palm facing upwards.

6. Repeat movements 4 and 5 two more times for a total of three times.

7. Thrust the Right hand forward into a level Biu Jee Strike.

8. Close the Right hand into a Ping Choi position.

9. Pull the Right hand back toward the Right shoulder and execute a Right Kwa Choi.

10. Place the hand back at the waist.

11. Perform movements 2 through 10 with the Left hand.

12. Shift into a Left Gung Jeen Bo.

13. Bring both palms up to your shoulders and push them forward using isotonic movement.

14. Circle both hands downward then up toward the shoulder and repeat movement 13 two more times.

15. Thrust both hands forward into a Cern Biu Jee Strike.

16. Close both hands into a Cern Ping Choi position.

17. Pull both fists back towards your shoulder rolling them over into a Cern Kwa Choi.

18. Pull both hands back to your waist.

19. Shift back to the Sei Ping Ma.

20. Shift into a right Gung Jeen Bo.

21. Perform movements 13 through 18 on the opposite side of the body.

22. Shift back to the Sei Ping Ma position.

23. Perform a Cern Biu Jee Strike downward at 45 degrees.

24. Execute a Cern Mei Yun Jiu Geang.

25. Move both hands to the left side of the chest both palms facing upwards right palm over the left.

26. Move both hands to the Right side of the chest and rotate the hands so that the Left palm faces downward and the Right palm faces inward.

27. Using Isotonic movement pushes both palms forward. (Be sure not to lock or hyper-extend your elbow.)

28. Repeat movements 25 through 27 two more times for a total of three times.

29. Perform the Plum Flower blocking maneuver circling the Right hand outward away from the body followed by the Left hand circling outward away from the body. (Each hand performs this maneuver 3 times for a total of 6 movements.)

30. After completing the Plum Flower blocking maneuver, place both hands on the Right side of the chest palms facing upwards with the Left hand over the Right Hand.

31. Move both hands from the Right side of the chest to the Left and rotate the hands so that the Right palm faces downward and the Left palm faces inward.

32. Repeat movements 25 through 27 on the other side of the body two more times for a total of three times.

33. Remain in the Sei Ping Ma position and flip the Right hand outward while at the same time rotating the Left hand outward.

34. Pull both hands back toward the body in a downward circling motion bringing both palms up to the shoulder and using isotonic movement push them away from the body.

35. Repeat movement 34 two more times for a total of three times.

36. Circle both hands to the Left side of the body bringing them back to the chest. (Be sure to open your hands as wide as possible.)

37. Using more of your Chi to control your actions rather than isotonic movement push both hands forward closing them into a Cern Fu Jow.

38. Perform movements 36 and 37 again first to the Right, Left and Right again for a total of four times.

39. Roll both hands back to the waist.

40. Close out the Sei Ping Ma position.

41. Relax in the neutral position and the set is complete.

Chapter Four: Gei Bon Keun
Primary Fist

4

PRIMARY FIST

The Jow Ga system of Chinese martial arts is one of the most popular styles of kung fu in the world with schools not only in China and the United States but in countries as far away as Brazil, Poland, Australia Vietnam, Malaysia, Singapore, England, and Germany just to name a few.

One of the unique aspects of the system is the balance between hand and leg techniques as opposed to many other styles of kung fu which are divided between either strong hand techniques or powerful leg maneuvers. This difference in approach has lead to the famous phrase Southern hands, Northern legs (Nan Kuen Bok Toi) which describes just how different Southern style kung fu is from its Northern cousin.

Southern style practitioners who herald from the Guangdong or Fujian region of Southern China are generally not very tall and have very little space to maneuver. So the majority of their techniques are hand oriented such as fists, palms and various clawing maneuvers. Southern stylists leave out many of the jumping, spinning or aerial type kicks as they are viewed as techniques too risky to execute in life or death combat situations.

Practitioners of northern styles who originate from the Beijing or Shantung area of China, for example, are generally taller in height and have a greater amount of space in which to practice their art. So, the use of legs is much more common place than for the southern style practitioners. Also, the fact that the legs and in particular the quadriceps are the largest and strongest muscles in the human body make kicking techniques naturally more powerful on average than hand techniques.

Jow Lung, who is considered the main founder of the Jow Ga system, clearly understood the value of combining both schools of Chinese martial arts. Lung put the best of both worlds together in order to create a style that is well balanced in its application of hand and foot techniques.

When I began teaching for myself in the early1990's, I came to realize that the Jow Ga system was very right hand oriented. While well balanced in its application of technique, there were certain key maneuvers that were only executed on the right side of the body. For example, the technique known as Single Leg Flying Crane (Darn Toi Fei Hok), which is a combination technique employing a front Snap Kick to the groin and double Crane Wing strike to the eyes is performed only on the right side of the body. So, in 2005 I created three forms that would help to strengthen the left side of the body. This addresses the issue and assists in preventing what is known in the fitness industry as muscular imbalance. This is when the body can only perform certain maneuvers on one side and not the other without some difficulty.

The first of these three forms is called Gei Bon Kuen, which translates as Primary Fist and is quite helpful in the training of a potential student. This is due to the fact that this form, while shorter than most of the forms taught within Jow Ga, teaches the student how to execute key techniques on both the left and right sides of the body. This in turn makes the student more ambidextrous and well balanced in their movement. The student will also get a feel for the type of footwork referred to as Ten Shape Stepping (Sup Jee Bo). This footwork is used in most southern long range styles of kung fu where the practitioner's footwork will generally follow the direction of north, south, west, and east. Also, the student will, without realizing it, write out the Chinese character for the number 10 with their footwork as the number 10 in Chinese resembles the English mathematical sign for addition.

An additional distinguishing characteristic of the Primary Fist set is that the footwork is a bit more active and represents the Choy Ga side of the system. This aspect calls for the learner to advance and retreat on an opponent with greater frequency. In turn, the movement requires the student to shift quickly from one stance to another while employing very aggressive hand techniques. In one such sequence a practitioner will go from Kup Choi, to Woo Dip Sao, to Tek Toi, to Jit Fu Choi, to Sow Choi, to Jong Choi (Stamping Fist, to Butterfly Hands, to Snap Kick, to Tiger Intercepting Fist, to Round House Punch, to Short Upper Cut).

It is my hope that the beginner's learning of this set will make their journey into the study of the Jow Ga system easier and less confusing. As for the advanced student, Gei Bon Kuen will without a doubt give them the balance they need and provide them with greater options in the application of their techniques.

1. Stand in the Ready position

2. Bend both knees slightly and thrust both hands out to the side in a Biu Jee Strike.

3. Swing both arms inward toward the chest into a Double Ridge Hand Strike.

4. Close both hands into a Cern Ping Choi position.

5. Pull both hands back toward the shoulder.

6. Roll both fists over into a Cern Kwa Choi position.

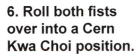  

7. Pull both hands back to the waist.

8. Step out into a Right Nau Ma while executing a Right Rising Block.

9. Move into a Left Sei Ping Ma and perform a Left Kum Sao.

10. Shift into a Left Gung Jeen Bo and execute a Right Biu Jee with the palm facing upwards.

11. Remain in a Left Gung Jeen Bo and perform a Rising Cross Block.

12. Shift into a Left Sei Ping Ma and perform a Cern Hok Yik.

13. Take a Half step with your Right foot and perform a Left Pak Sao.

14. Shift into a Left Diu Ma and salute once to the center.

15. Remain in Left Diu Ma and close both hands into a Cern Ping Choi.

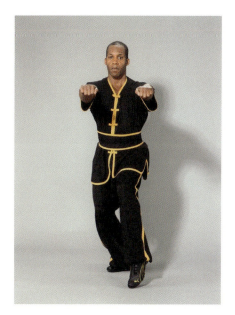 

16. Pull both hands back towards the shoulder.

17. Roll both fists over into a Cern Kwa Choi.

18. Pull both fists back to the waist and stand up into the Ready position.

19. Open to the Sei Ping Ma position.

20. Half Step on the Right Heel to a Left Gung Jeen Bo and execute a Right Ping Choi.

21. Pull back into a Left Diu Ma and perform the first portion of the Jiu Sao technique.

22. Remain in the Diu Ma position and complete the Jiu Sao technique.

23. Shift forward into a Left Gung Jeen Bo and attack with a Right Ping Choi.

24. Step forward into a Right Gung Jeen Bo executing a Left Pak Sao finishing with a Right Kwa Choi.

25. Pull back into a Right Diu Ma and block with a Left Hok Yik.

FRONT VIEW

26. Shift forward to a Right Sei Ping Ma and strike with a Right Yum Chop Choi to the rib cage.

27. Twist into a Right Nau Ma and perform a Left Kup Choi.

28. Step forward to a Left Gung Jeen Bo and attack with a Right Pow Choi.

29. Turn 180 degrees to the Right to a Right Gung Jeen Bo and Inside Block finishing with a Left Ping Choi.

30. Perform movements 21 up to 28 in the opposite direction.

FRONT VIEW

31. Shift to your Left 90 degrees into a Left side Gung Jeen Bo and attack with a right Kup Choi Strike.

32. Remain at 90 degrees and bring the Right foot up into a Right Diu Ma position while at the same time performing a Right Woo Dip Sao both hands finishing on the Right side of the body.

33. Perform a Right Toe Kick.

34. Step down and behind into a Right Tau Ma and execute a Right Jit Fu Choi Block.

SIDE VIEW

35. Rotate 180 degrees to the Left into a Left Gung Jeen Bo attacking with a Right Sow Choi Punch.

36. Shift behind you 180 degrees into a Right Sei Ping Ma and execute a Right Jong Choi to the rib cage.

SIDE VIEW

37. Shift the Right foot back and to the Right 90 degrees into a Right side Gung Jeen Bo and strike with a Left Kup Choi.

38. Repeat movements 32 through 36 on the opposite side of the body.

SIDE VIEWS

SIDE VIEW

39. Shift into a Left Gung Jeen Bo and attack with a Right Cern Fu Jow.

40. Stepping to the Left into a Right Tau Ma perform the Woo Dip Sao. (Left hand in the Pak Sao position, Right hand in Hok Yik position.)

41. Step over the Right foot into a Left Nau Ma Stance raising both hands over the head.

42. Move into a Right Sei Ping Ma placing both hands on the Left side of the body.

43. Shift into a Right Gung Jeen Bo and attack with the Woo Dip Sao striking with the edge of both hands.

44. Perform movements 40 through 43 in the opposite direction.

45. Step with your Right foot to your Right at 45 degrees into a Right Gung Jeen Bo and execute a Lin Wan Choi. (The Right hand blocking and the Left hand punching.)

46. Repeat movement 45 on the Left side of the body stepping 45 degrees to the Left into a Left Gung Jeen Bo.

47. Execute movement 45 once more this time stepping straight ahead at 90 degrees into a Right Gung Jeen Bo.

48. Swinging the Right foot over the Left move into a Right Tau Ma position blocking downward with a Jit Fu Choi.

SIDE VIEW

49. Rotate 180 degrees to the Left into a Left Gung Jeen Bo and strike downward with a Right Kup Choi.

50. Shift into a Left Sei Ping Ma and execute a Cern Ping Jong.

SIDE VIEW

51. Remain in the Sei Ping Ma position and perform a Cern Hok Yik.

52. Take a half step with your Right foot and block with a Left Pak Sao.

53. Shift back into a Left Diu Ma and salute.

54. Remain in the Diu Ma position and strike out with a Cern Ping Choi.

55. Pull both fists back toward the shoulder.

56. Roll both fists over into a Cern Kwa Choi.

57. Pull both fist back to your waist stepping back into the Ready position and the form is complete.

APPLICATIONS

FIRST TECHNIQUE

1. Face each other
in the On Guard position.

2. Your opponent attacks
with a Right Ping Choi.

3. Step up quickly into a
Right Gung Jeen Bo position
and block with a Left Pak Sao
striking simultaneously with a
Right Kwa Choi.

4. Your opponent uses a Tiger
Claw grab stopping your attack.

5. Pull back into a Right Diu Ma while simultaneously breaking out of the grab using the Hok Yik Block.

6. As your opponent attempts another Right Ping Choi move into a Right Sei Ping Ma and block with a Left Pak Sao.

7. Finish the sequence by striking with a Right Yum Chop Choi to the ribs.

Second Technique

1. Start from the On Guard position.

2. Your opponent attacks with a Right Ping Choi.

3. Move forward quickly into a Right Diu Ma position and intercept the opponent's punch using the Woo Dip Sao technique immobilizing their attack.

4. Once the opponent is unable to move finish the sequence with a Right Front Snap Kick to the area of the groin.

Third Technique

1. Stand in a neutral position.

2. Your attacker grabs you by the Right shoulder.

3. Step back with your left foot dropping quickly into your Sei Ping Ma while using the first half of the Cern Fu Jow technique to trap and unbalance your opponent.

4. Shift quickly into a Right Gung Jeen Bo Stance and strike with the second half of the Cern Fu Jow technique.

Fourth Technique

1. Stand in the neutral position.

2. Your opponent grabs you by the Left wrist.

3. Roll your wrist outward away from the body and counter grab your adversary by their wrist while simultaneously twisting into a Left Nau Ma position.

4. As you continue moving into the Left Nau Ma position strike with a Right Kup Choi to the head of your opponent.

Chapter Five: Dai Fok Fu Kuen
Big Controlling Tiger Fist

Big Controlling Tiger Fist

The form known as Dai Fok Fu Kuen (Big Subduing Tiger Fist) is an original set within the Jow Ga system created at the time of Jow Lung's life. This form along with four other sets, Siu Fok Fu Kuen (Small Subduing Tiger Fist), Chai Jong Kuen (Fire Wood Post Fist), Fu Pow Kuen (Tiger Cougar Fist) and Man Jeet Kuen (10,000 Shape Fist) are essential for all practitioners of the Jow Ga system. These sets are referred to as seed forms meaning that the majority of the system is contained within these five sets.

Dai Fok Fu Kuen is referred to as a Chi building - Chi releasing form. This is due to the fact that the first half of the form which is very stationary contains a vast amount of Chi Gung practice through the use of isotonic movement. This movement when done in conjunction with proper breathing gives the Jow Ga practitioner tremendous power in both their offensive and defensive techniques. When first learning this set, it is common for the learner to tire quickly as he/she will normally use more of their muscular strength when practicing the Chi Gung section of the form. However, after constant training and a clear understanding of how to connect their physical movements with their breathing, the practitioner will notice that their ability to perform this half of the form, which in my opinion is the most demanding part of the set, has become easier due to the increase of Chi within the practitioner. The second half of the Dai Fok Fu form is all about fighting. Here the Jow Ga student will move quickly from one technique to another using maneuvers form both Northern and Southern Shaolin schools tapping into the wealth of knowledge that Jow Lung truly possessed. It is at this point that the Jow Ga student will tire for another reason as he/she will aggressively move from offense to defense without stopping. In one sequence the student will execute three standing sweeps in a row and then jump backwards away from their opponent landing in a Cross Stance while performing a Double Level Punch on either side of the body. So, as one can clearly see, learning the Dai Fok Fu set will not only improve your overall health, it will also give you a wealth of combat knowledge that can serve you well in almost any situation in which you may find yourself.

1. Stand in the ready position.

2. Bend both knees slightly and perform a Cern Poon Kiu.

3. Step forward into a Right Nau Ma circling the Right hand above the head and the Left hand by the Right waist.

4. Step forward into a Left Sei Ping Ma and perform a Left Kum Sao Block.

5. Shift into a Left Gung Jeen Bo while executing a Right Biu Jee with the palm facing upwards.

6. Step back into a Right Tau Ma and perform a High/Low Double Block.

7. Turn counterclockwise and execute a Right Tornado Kick landing in a Left Diu Ma and perform a Single Salute to the center.

8. Remain in the Diu Ma position and perform a Cern Ping Choi.

9. Pull both hands back to the shoulder.

10. Roll both fists over into a Cern Kwa Choi.

11. Pull both hands back to the waist and step back into the ready position.

12. Open to the Sei Ping Ma position.

13. Perform a Right downward Biu Jee Strike at 45 degrees.

14. Execute a Right Mei Yun Jiu Geang.

15. Turn the Right Palm upward cutting it across the chest from left to right.

16. Turn the palm outwards and using isotonic movement push the Right palm forward.

17. Repeat movements 15 and 16 two more times for a total of three repetitions.

18. Pull the Right hand upwards placing the Right elbow close to the Right ear.

19. Execute a Right downward Fu Jow finishing with the hand at the waist.

20. Thrust out a Right handed Biu Jee.

21. Remain in the Square Sei Ping Ma position and perform a Half step with your Right foot and execute the first half of the Woo Dip Sao.

22. Shift into a Left Gung Jeen Bo and strike out with both hands with the second half of the Woo Dip Sao.

23. Move into a Right Sei Ping Ma and striking with a Right Don Lon.

24. Throw a Left Ping Choi from the Square Sei Ping Ma position.

25. Pull the Left hand back towards the shoulder and strike with a Left Kwa Choi.

26. Pull the Left hand back to the waist.

27. Repeat movements 13 through 26 on the other side of the body.

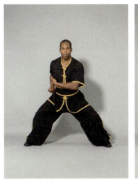    

28. Remain in the Sei Ping Ma position taking a Half step with the Right foot and execute a Left Kum Sao Block.

29. Continue moving into a Left Gung Jeen Bo and strike downward with a Right Biu Jee.

30. Remain in Left Gung Jeen Bo position performing a Left Pak Sao, Right Kwa Jeung combination. (Hands should move in a circular motion.)

31. Turn sharply 180 degrees to the right into a Right Gung Jeen Bo Stance and perform a simultaneous Right Hok Yik Strike and Left Pak Sao Block.

32. Perform the Moi Fa blocking maneuver while remaining in the Gung Jeen Bo position. (Perform the blocking maneuver 3 to 5 times.)

33. Shift back into a Right Diu Ma position pulling both hands to the Left waist.

34. Step forward into a Right Gung Jeen Bo and push both palms forward using isotonic movement.

35. Repeat movement 34 two more times for total of three times.

36. Remain in the Gung Jeen Bo Stance and pull both hands back and upwards.

37. Claw downward with both hands while pulling back into a Right Diu Ma.

38. Shift forward back into the Right Gung Jeen Bo and execute a Cern Biu Jee.

39. Close both hands into the Ping Choi position and shift quickly to the Sei Ping Ma position and bring both hands to your shoulders.

40. Roll both fists over into a Cern Kwa Choi.

41. Pull both hands back to the waist.

42. Remain in the Sei Ping Ma position and execute a Left half step and Right Kum Sao Block.

43. Continue shifting into a Right Gung Jeen Bo and strike with a down ward Left Biu Jee Strike at 45 degrees.

44. Remain in a Right Gung Jeen Bo and perform a Right Pak Sao and Left Kwa Jeung. (Hands should move in a rotating fashion.)

45. Shift sharply 180 degrees to the left into a Left Gung Jeen Bo and perform a simultaneous Left Hok Yik Strike and Right Pak Sao Block.

46. Perform movements 32 through 38 on the opposite side of the body.

47. Turn swiftly 180 degrees to the right into a Right Gung Jeen Bo and attack with a Left Sow Choi Punch.

48. Half step with the right foot while performing a circular block with the Left hand finishing with a Right Ping Choi in the Right Sei Ping Ma Stance.

49. Shift into a square Sei Ping Ma position and perform a Right Hook Punch.

50. Remain in square Sei Ping Ma position and strike with a Right Kwa Choi.

51. Pull the right hand back to the waist.

52. Swing the right leg over the left and stand in a right side ready position.

53. Using a running step move quickly into a Left Sei Ping Ma at 45 degrees and execute a Cern Kwa Choi.

54. Half step with your right foot and shift into a Left Gung Jeen Bo while performing a downward Right Biu Jee Strike at 45 degrees.

55. Remain in the Left Gung Jeen Bo position and execute a Right Mei Yun Jiu Geang.

56. Bring the right hand across the chest from left to right and push the palm forward using isotonic movement.

57. Perform these movements two more times for a total of three times.

58. Pull the right arm upwards toward your right ear.

59. While shifting into a Left Diu Ma Stance claw downward with a Right Darn Fu Jow.

60. Shift forward into a Left Gung Jeen Bo and strike with a Right Biu Jee.

61. Move into a Left Sei Ping Ma position while performing the Jiu Sao technique finishing with a Right Ping Choi.

62. Move into a square Sei Ping Ma Stance and perform a Left Poon Kiu Block.

63. Remain in the square Sei Ping Ma and execute a Left Rising Block at 45 degrees.

64. Shift into Right Gung Jeen Bo while performing a Left Cutting Palm to the ribs.

65. Move back into a Left Sei Ping Ma striking with a Left Don Lon.

66. Execute a Right Ping Choi while in Sei Ping Ma position.

67. Pull the right hand back to the shoulder.

68. Strike with a Right Kwa Choi.

69. Pull the right hand back to the waist.

70. Swing the left leg over the right and stand up to the Left side ready position.

71. Perform movements 53 through 69 on the opposite side of the body.

72. Swing the right leg over the left and stand up into a Right side ready position.

73. Perform a Right Snap Kick followed by a Double Jumping Snap Kick.

74. Land in a Right Gung Jeen Bo and execute a Double Palm Strike.

75. Pullback into a Right Diu Ma and perform a Cern Hok Yik Block.

76. Step over to your right 90 degrees into a Left Diu Ma position and grabbing with a Left Fu Jow and strike with a Right Fung Ngam Choi.

SIDE VIEW

77. Shift forward into a Right Sei Ping Ma and strike with a Right Don Lon.

78. Execute a Right Tornado Kick.

79. Land from the kick into a Right Sei Ping Ma and perform a circular Hooking Block with your left hand and finish with a Right Ping Choi.

80. Step around counter clockwise to your left finishing in a Left Sei Ping Ma position and execute the Jiu Sao maneuver finishing with a Right Ping Choi in a Left Gung Jeen Bo position.

FRONT VIEW

 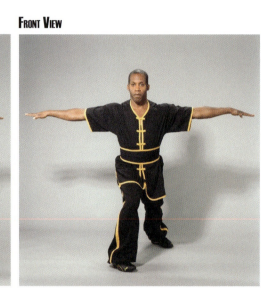

81. Remain in the Left Gung Jeen Bo Stance and cross your arms Right over Left.

82. Turn around 180 degrees to your right into a Right Gung Jeen Bo and strike with a Cern Don Lon.

83. Step 45 degrees to your left into a Left Sei Ping Ma and execute the Jiu Sao technique finishing with a Right Ping Choi.

FRONT VIEW

84. Using a Running step move 45 degrees to your right into a Left Nau Ma and execute a Right Ping Jong.

85. Continue moving to your right into a Right Sei Ping Ma at 45 degrees and perform maneuver 83 on the other side of the body.

FRONT VIEWS

86. Drop down to your left into a Left side Lok Quie Ma position and perform a Right Jong Choi to the groin.

87. Stand up and shift into a Right side Gung Jeen Bo and Left Scissors Block.

88. Shift back to your left and perform a Right Sow Gek to your opponent's leg and Right Don Lon Strike to the throat.

89. Perform maneuver number 88 with your Left leg and then your Right leg for a total of three times.

90. Jump backwards into a Right Tau Ma Stance and strike to both the left and right sides of the body with a Ping Choi.

91. While rotating to your left execute a Left Hooking Block finishing the maneuver in a Right Sei Ping Ma and Right Ping Choi.

92. Move into a Right Tau Ma position while performing the Moi Fa blocking technique.

93. Rotate 180 degrees to your left into a Left Gung Jeen Bo Stance and striking with a Right Sow Choi.

94. Start with standing Right Jit Fu Choi while simultaneously executing a 90 degree Jump Turn to your right landing in a Right Lok Quie Ma position and perform a Left Jit Fu Choi.

95. Slide to your left into a Left Lok Quie Ma Stance and strike with a Right Jong Choi to the groin.

96. Repeat maneuver 87.

97. Shift to your left and perform a Right Sow Gek, Don Lon maneuver.

98. Perform maneuver 97 again on the opposite side of the body.

99. Shift into a Left side Gun Jeen Bo and strike with a Right Biu Jong.

100. Shift to your right into a Right side Gung Jeen Bo attacking with a Left Biu Jong.

101. Move into a Left side Diu Ma Stance grabbing with a Left Fu Jow and striking with a simultaneous Right Fung Ngam Choi to the temple.

102. Step forward into a Left Nau Ma position striking with downward Kwa Choi placing the right hand into the palm of the left hand.

103. Execute a Cern Hok Yik Block and Right Front Snap Kick.

104. Step down into a Right Sei Ping Ma and execute a Left Hooking Block finishing with a Right Ping Choi.

105. Step to a Right Tau Ma while executing the Moi Fa blocking technique.

106. Rotate 180 degrees to your left into a Left Gung Jeen Bo Stance and strike with a Right Sow Choi.

107. Jump and turn 180 degrees to your right landing in a Right Lok Quie Ma position while executing a Left Jit Fu Choi.

108. Repeat movements 95 through 106 in the same exact order as before.

109. Step with your right foot over your left into a Right Nau Ma crossing your arms in front of your chest.

110. Move into a Square Sei Ping Ma position with your palms facing outward from the Shoulder.

111. Push your hands outward to the side using isotonic movement while shuffling to the left in the Sei Ping Ma Stance. (Perform this movement a total of three times.)

112. Remain in Sei Ping Ma position and lift both hands upward toward your ears.

113. Drop both hands downward toward your waist.

114. Shuffle to your right once while still in the Sei Ping Ma position and strike outward to the both left and right sides with Biu Jee Strike.

115. Remain in the Sei Ping Ma and strike with a Cern Jong Choi to the ribs.

116. Take a Half step with your right foot and perform the first half of the Woo Dip Sao.

117. Shift into a Left Gung Jeen Bo position and strike toward the ribs with the second half of the Woo Dip Sao.

118. Move your right foot up to a 90 degree position into a Right Sei Ping Ma and execute a Right Hok Yik Block.

119. Perform the Jiu Sao maneuver finishing with a Left Ping Choi in Right Gung Jeen Bo position.

120. Slide your right foot back to a Square Sei Ping Ma Stance while performing a Left Pak Sao Block.

121. Repeat maneuvers 116 through 119 on the other side of the body.

122. Slide the left foot back into a Right side Gung Jeen Bo while executing a Left Scissors Block.

123. Shift over to your left and execute a Right Sow Gek, Right Don Lon combination.

124. Move into a Right Tau Ma position and perform the Moi Fa blocking maneuver.

125. Rotate 180 degrees to your left into a Left Gung Jeen Bo and attack with a Right Sow Choi.

126. Shift and turn 180 degrees to your right into a Right Gung Jeen Bo while performing a Left Pow Choi.

REVERSE VIEW

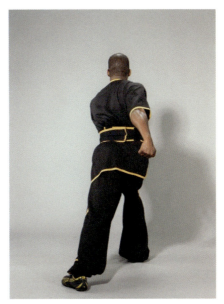

127. Step to your right at 45 degrees into a Left Nau Ma and execute a Double Inverted Palm Block.

128. Step forward into a Right Gung Jeen Bo position and execute a Double Palm Strike to the mid-section.

129. Remain at the 45 degree position and slide back into a Right Sei Ping Ma Stance and block downward with a Single Inverted Palm Block.

130. Execute the Jiu Sao technique finishing with a Left Half step into a Right Gung Jeen Bo Stance and Left Ping Choi.

REVERSE VIEWS

REVERSE VIEW

131. Step 45 degrees your left into a Left Gung Jeen Bo Stance and while attacking with a Right Kup Choi Strike.

132. Repeat maneuvers 127 up to 130 on the opposite side of the body.

Reverse Views

133. Shift your body into a Right side Gung Jeen Bo Stance at 90 degrees and execute a Left Scissors Block.

134. Execute a Right Sow Gek, Right Don Lon combination.

135. Move into a Right Sei Ping Ma position and strike with a Right Jong Choi.

136. Turn 180 degrees to your left into a Left Gung Jeen Bo position striking with a Right Sow Choi Punch.

137. Shift into a Left Sei Ping Ma Stance and execute a Cern Ping Jong.

138. Push both hands outward to the side away from the body using isotonic movement.

SIDE VIEWS

139. Drop both hands downward into the Hok Yik position.

140. Perform a Left Pak Sao while taking a Half Step with your Right foot.

141. Salute to your center in a Left Diu Ma Stance.

142. Perform maneuvers 8 through 11 and the form is complete.

APPLICATIONS
FIRST TECHNIQUE

1. Stand in a neutral position.

2. Your opponent grabs the lapel of your garment.

3. Step back into the Diu Ma position and execute a Cern Hok Yik Block which breaks the grip of your opponent.

4. From this point counter grab your opponent by the wrist and finish with a Front Snap Kick to the groin.

Second Technique

1. Face each other in the On Guard position.

2. Your opponent attacks with a Right Ping Choi.

3. Intercept your opponent's attack with a Left Kum Sao.

4. Shift into a Left Gung Jeen Bo and counter attack with a Right Biu Jee to the groin.

5. Your opponent shifts into a Sei Ping Ma position and blocks with his own Kum Sao.

6. Trap the blocking hand quickly with a Left Pak Sao.

7. Finish the sequence by attacking with a Right Kwa Jeung to the head of the opponent.

THIRD TECHNIQUE

1. Face each other in the On Guard position.

2. Your opponent attacks with a Right Front Snap Kick.

3. Twist into a Left Nau Ma position and intercept with a Double Inverted Palm Block.

4. Step forward into a Right Gung Jeen Bo position and strike with Double Palm Strike to the mid-section.

Fourth Technique

1. Face each other in the On Guard position.

2. Attack your opponent with a Right Ping Choi.

3. Your opponent counters with a Left Hok Yik Block.

4. He then attacks with his own Right Ping Choi.

5. Remain in a Left Gung Jeen Bo and block with a Rising Elbow Block.

6. Shift your weight back into a Left Diu Ma position grabbing your opponent's wrist with a Darn Fu Jow.

7. Shift your weight forward into your Left Gung Jeen Bo Stance and attack with a Biu Jee Strike to the throat of your opponent.

8. Finish with a Left Hok Yik Strike to the eyes from a Left Sei Ping Ma Stance.

Chapter Six: Moi Fah Cheung
Plum Blossom Spear

Plum Blossom Spear

One of the unique aspects of the Chinese martial arts is the vast amount of weapons that can be learned as one goes through their training. Depending on the style, a student could learn as few as two such as the case in the Ip Man branch of the Wing Chun system that teaches the 6 ½ Point Pole forms and the Eight Chopping Knives (Butterfly Knives) set. Or a student could learn as many as 20 or more if he/she were to study from one of the many branches of the Choy Li Fut system. Whatever one's personal preference in terms of style, the mastery of what many teachers consider to be the four main weapons of Chinese kung fu is essential for any and all looking to further their knowledge and experience of the Chinese martial arts.

The Guan (Pole), Darn Dao (Broad Sword), Gim (Straight Sword), and Cheung (Spear) are the four main weapons that most kung fu stylists, regardless of the system, must master before other more advanced weapons can be learned. Of these four weapons, many masters regard the spear to be the king of weapons as it takes on many of the traits of the other three without losing its own identity. Within this one weapon, you have the hard striking power of the pole, the cutting and slashing traits of the broad sword, and the smooth but direct thrusting ability of the straight sword.

Spear tactics require the practitioner to be of a relaxed and calm nature as speed is essential in the execution and application the techniques. The tactical application of the spear can also quickly transform as the practitioner can maneuver this weapon from long range techniques to short range maneuvers in an instant. For example, an exponent can go from the technique Sau Hau Cheung (Locking Throat Spear) striking an adversary in the throat from a kneeling position to the technique Hong (Blowing the Flute) attacking an opponent with a strike to the head using the shaft of the weapon.

The Moi Fah Cheung or Plum Blossom Spear set is an original form taught within the Jow Ga system. Like most spear forms the performer must have a power that is both relaxed and smooth. But, because Jow Ga is a blend of Northern and Southern Shaolin martial arts, the Plum Blossom Spear should be performed with both hard and soft energies (Gong Ging/Yow Ging). This means that when parrying a strike, it is important that the Jow Ga practitioner use a more flexible type of energy. But when striking an adversary, they should use a more forceful type of energy that is meant to crush your opponent with a single strike.

In this text, this version of the Moi Fah Cheung comes from the Dean Chin branch of the Jow Ga system and is visibly shorter than the version he had learned while training with Grand Master Chan Man Cheung in Hong Kong. This is due to the fact that Sifu Chin wanted to get his American students caught up to their Asian counterparts as quickly as possible. By cutting out many of the repetitious movements performed within the form, he was able to maintain the integrity of the form and achieve his goal of teaching the true essence of the Jow Ga system to his American students who to this day carry on the legacy of the founder of Jow Ga kung fu in America.

Spear Techniques and Drills

Although known as a long range weapon, the Spear (Cheung) is extremely varied in its usage. For example, one can use the tip of the weapon, the full length of the shaft, and even the butt end of the weapon against an opponent. Speed and proper footwork are just a few of the attributes needed in order to excel in the usage of the spear.

While commonly viewed as a weapon practiced by many Northern kung fu stylists, Southern stylists also place great value in the usage of one of kung fu's most cherished weapons. With a country as diverse as China, one can only assume that the methods of using the spear between Northern and Southern styles of kung fu would be as well.

This diversity, however, is not just demonstrated in the techniques of the weapon, but in the way power is manifested. The power displayed in Northern style spear techniques tends to be of a more fluid nature similar to that of the Straight Sword (Gim). Southern style spear techniques lend themselves to being of a more forceful nature where the power is more direct in its application similar to the Southern style staff (Guan).

Weather your chosen style of kung fu is from the north or the south, the techniques of the spear are shared almost equally by both factions of Chinese martial arts. The following is a list of maneuvers taught within the Moi Fah Cheung set. Although there are many more maneuvers that are associated with the use of this weapon, the author only wishes to teach those techniques that are directly related to this form as it was taught by Master Dean Chin at the time of his life.

Techniques of the Plum Blossom Spear

Cheung
This is the most basic of techniques. Holding the spear by the butt end with both hands the practitioner shoots the weapon forward in a stabbing motion toward the chest of the opponent.

Nah
This block is performed on the lower left side of the body at an angle of 45 degrees.

Kum
A downward circular block designed to parry the opponent's weapon.

HONG
Sometimes called "Blowing the Flute" is performed by extending both hands outward striking with the shaft of the spear.

DIK SOY
Known as "Dripping Water" is performed by the practitioner raising the spear above their head at a position of 45 degrees with the blade of the spear pointing downwards.

SAU HOW CHEUNG
Referred to as "Locking Throat Spear" this maneuver is generally performed from the Lok Quie Ma "Kneeling Stance" and is designed to strike an adversary in the area of the throat from underneath their guard.

DA SIU KEI

"Hit with a Small Flag" is a spinning type of maneuver designed to strike the adversary horizontally across the body or head.

SOT

This is a downward strike which uses the waist of the practitioner to generate power.

LAU

A slicing Upper Cut Strike executed from the Gung Jeen Bo (Bow and Arrow) Stance position.

Drills and Exercises

Once you've had a chance to learn the individual techniques of the spear, the next step is to practice these maneuvers in a combination of both offensive and defensive applications. Within this text there will be two exercises taught to help you develop your skill with the spear.

Saam Look: Three Skills

In this drill, three of the most essential techniques are combined into a smooth and fluid exercise designed to teach the practitioner the basics of how to handle the weapon.

1. Start from a Right Sei Ping Ma Stance holding the spear in the On Guard position.

2. Shift your weight into a Reverse Gung Jeen Bo executing the Nah blocking maneuver.

3. Move back into your Right Sei Ping Ma Stance and circle block downward using the Kum technique.

4. Shift forward into a Right Gung Jeen Bo and perform a Level Cheung thrusting technique.

Practice this exercise for a minimum of 20 repetitions with 3 movements equaling 1 rep. Also, be sure to coordinate your breathing with your movement, exhaling outward in both the defensive and offensive technique.

Bot Cheung Faht: Eight Spear Method

This exercise is designed to not only teach you the mechanics of using the spear, but how to employ the proper footwork in order to position yourself in relationship to your opponent so that their defenses will be exposed to your attack.

1. Start from the On Guard position.

2. Shift into a Left Side Gung Jeen Bo position executing a downward Nah Block.

3. Step into a Right Sei Ping Ma while performing the Kum blocking technique.

4. Shift into a Right Gung Jeen Bo position and attack with a Level Cheung Strike.

Front View

5. Turn 180 degrees to your left into a Left Gung Jeen Bo Stance and strike downward using the Sot maneuver.

6. Jump and spin 360 degrees around d to your right landing in a Right Lok Quie Ma position and attack using the Saw How Cheung technique.

7. Stand up and shift into a Left Reverse Gung Jeen Bo Stance and block over head using the Dik Soy maneuver.

8. Shift to a Right Sei Ping Ma Stance and circle block downward using the Kum technique.

9. Move into a Right Gung Jeen Bo position and strike outward using a Level Cheung.

When practicing the Eight Spear Method exercise, it is important to coordinate your breathing with your movement by exhaling on both offensive and defensive techniques. Also, the rooting of your stance combined with the flexibility of your waist will give your spear techniques both power and fluidity.

FLOATING

This exercise is designed to increase the gripping power of the hands and the strengthening of your wrist. By practicing this exercise you will be able to handle the spear with greater ease and effectiveness. The exercise also carries with it an added feature with the improvement of your Chin Na (Control and Seize) techniques making it easier to maintain a firm grip on your adversary's joints should you need to employ these techniques in a self defense situation.

1. Begin by sitting in the Sei Ping Ma position holding the spear by the butt end in front of your chest with your right hand. (Spear must be parallel to the floor.)

2. Rotate the spear outward away from the body, keeping the tip of the weapon directly in front of the chest while allowing the shaft to be positioned at an angle of 45 degrees.

3. Slowly rotate your spear back inward toward your chest and the exercise is complete.

After performing the exercise anywhere from 10 to 20 repetitions, repeat the same sequence with your left hand. When performing this drill be sure to coordinate your breathing with your movement so that you are exhaling on the active part of the exercise and inhaling on the passive part of the exercise.

SHAKING

Ging is the physical manifestation of Chi. Ging is the ability to take the Chi or energy you have developed and channel it to any one part of your body such as a hand or foot and direct it outward. This means from a combat standpoint that an unsuspecting opponent will be the recipient of this massive amount of focused energy. The Shaking exercise is a great way to develop your Ging. Your Ging can be harnessed while practicing with the spear and can be applied in empty hand combat.

1. Begin by sitting in the Sei Ping Ma position holding the spear at the butt end in both hands with the weapon parallel to the floor.

2. Slam both hands downward forcefully while exhaling at the same time which will cause the spear to shake. The position of the shaft should be 45 degrees.

3. Bring the hands up to the starting position and repeat again.

When performing this exercise be sure to inhale as you bring your weapon back up into the starting position. Also, using brute strength to perform the exercise may cause you to hyper-extend the elbow. So, be sure that you are using a combination of both physical strength and internal power when performing this exercise.

NOTE: This exercise can also be performed one handed. Perform the drill in the same manner as the two handed version concentrating on just one hand at a time.

Plum Blossom Spear

Side View

1. Stand with your feet together holding the Spear in both hands with the tip of your weapon on the right side of your body.

2. Bend your knees slightly and raise the spear up chest level.

Side View

3. Move into a Right foot forward Nau Ma Stance and with a swinging motion attack the head of your opponent with the butt end of the spear.

Side View

4. Step into a Left foot forward Gung Jeen Bo Stance and strike with a Lau Cheung.

5. Hop in place into a Left Diu Ma position while swinging the spear over your Left shoulder finishing with the spear held vertically in your Left hand and saluting with your Right hand in an open palm position.

FRONT VIEWS

SIDE VIEWS

6. Remain in the Left Diu Ma Stance and close the Right hand into a Ping Choi position.

7. Pull the Right hand back to the shoulder.

8. Roll the Right fist over into the Kwa Choi position.

9. Pull the Right hand back to your waist and stand up into the ready position.

SIDE VIEW   SIDE VIEW

10. Step back into a Left reverse Gung Jeen Bo Stance and perform a Nah Block.

SIDE VIEW

11. Shift into Right Sei Ping Ma and perform the Kum Cheung blocking maneuver.

12. Move into a Right Gung Jeen Bo and strike with a level Cheung to the chest of your opponent.

13. Repeat movements 10 through 12 once more in the same sequence.

14. Step up and forward to your Left at 45 degrees into a Left Gung Jeen Bo position and attack the chest using the Hong technique.

15. Step to your Right at 45 degrees into a Right Sei Ping Ma and execute a short range Cheung technique toward the head of your opponent.

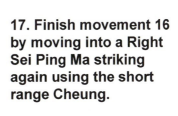

16. Remain at 45 degrees and step into a Left Nau Ma position while at the same time using a clockwise circling technique to parry the weapon of your opponent.

17. Finish movement 16 by moving into a Right Sei Ping Ma striking again using the short range Cheung.

18. Perform a parrying technique to your Left while at the same time hop back away from your opponent at 45 degrees to your Left finishing in a Right Single Leg Stance and strike with an upward Cheung technique toward the throat.

SIDE VIEWS

SIDE VIEW

19. Step down into a Left foot reverse Gung Jeen Bo Stance and execute a Dik Soy Block.

20. Slide down into a Right Lok Quie Ma position and strike with the Saw Hau Cheung toward the throat of your opponent.

21. Step forward into a Left Gung Jeen Bo Stance and execute an Over Head Block.

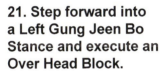

22. Turn to your right into a Right Sei Ping Ma position and use the Da Siu Kei technique to attack your opponent's mid-section.

23. Stand up and twist to your Left 360 degrees moving through a Left Nau Ma into a Left Gung Jeen Bo Stance while at the same time spinning the spear vertically finishing with a Lau Cheung.

SIDE VIEWS (STEP 23)

24. Move quickly from Right Nau Ma to Left Gung Jeen Bo striking first with the butt end of the spear and finishing with the Lau Cheung technique

25. Take two to four steps forward while rotating the spear vertically using this maneuver to both attack your opponent and deflect any incoming attack.
(This technique is called Flowering.)

SIDE VIEW

26. At the end of your second or fourth step execute a Right front Snap Kick and downward Cheung to the rear attacking the leg of your opponent.

27. Step back down into a Left foot forward Gung Jeen Bo and perform the Sot Cheung technique to the head of your adversary.

28. Jump and spin 360 degrees to your right landing in a Right Lok Quie Ma position while executing the Saw Hau Cheung technique.

29. Stand up into a Left Reverse Gung Jeen Bo position and execute the Dik Soy blocking technique.

30. Shift into a Right Sei Ping Ma and parry downward with the Kum Cheung technique.

31. Move into a Right Gung Jeen Bo and strike forward with a level Cheung maneuver.

SIDE VIEW

SIDE VIEW

32. Turn 180 degrees to the left into a Left Gung Jeen Bo and perform the Sot Cheung.

33. Repeat movements 3 and 4 that are seen in the beginning of the form.

34. Repeat maneuvers 25 through 31 in the same exact order.

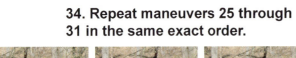

SIDE VIEWS

35. Shift into a Right Diu Ma at 45 degrees to your right and block a low line attack to the leg with the butt end of the spear.

36. Flower the spear into a Nah blocking position while simultaneously hooking the right leg behind the left leg.

37. Remain at 45 degrees and step down into a Right Sei Ping Ma parrying downward with the Kum Cheung technique.

38. Shift into a Right Gung Jeen Bo Stance performing a Level Cheung maneuver.

39. Step with your right foot at 45 degrees into a Right Gung Jeen Bo and strike horizontally with the butt end of the spear.

40. Step forward into a Left Gung Jeen Bo Stance striking with the Lau Cheung technique.

SIDE VIEWS

41. Repeat movements 25 through 27.

42. Jump and turn to your right 360 degrees and land in a Right Gung Jeen Bo Stance and strike with a Level Cheung technique.

43. Repeat movement 27.

44. Slide the left foot back into the Sei Ping Ma position and jab forward with the butt end of the spear.

45. Move the left foot forward into a Left Gung Jeen Bo Stance and strike upward using the Lau Cheung technique.

46. Repeat movements 3 and 4.

47. Repeat maneuvers 25 through 27 ending with maneuver 42.

48. Take your right foot stepping across the body at 45 degrees to your left into a Right Nau Ma position and jab with the butt end of the spear.

49. Remain at 45 degrees stepping the Left foot back over the Right moving quickly into a Right Sei Ping Ma position finishing with the downward Kum Cheung maneuver.

50. Shift into a Right Gung Jeen Bo and execute a Cheung Strike.

51. Repeat maneuvers 48 through 50 three more times for a total of four times. Be sure each time to step toward your left shoulder first at a position of 45 degrees.

52. Shift to your Left at 45 degrees moving into a Right Diu Ma position while at the same time circle parry your opponent's weapon counterclockwise finishing with the Kum Cheung maneuver in Right Diu Ma.

53. Step into a Right Gung Jeen Bo Stance and attack with the Level Cheung maneuver.

54. Repeat movement 27.

55. Move forward into a Right Diu Ma Stance performing the Kum Cheung maneuver at the same time.

56. Repeat movement 53.

57. Step back with your right foot over your left into a Right Tau Ma position while performing a clockwise circle parry block.

58. Rotate 180 degrees to the left into a Left Gung Jeen Bo and jab with the butt end of the spear. (The spear should be tucked underneath the right arm.)

59. Remain in the Left Gung Jeen Bo position and repeat movement 27.

60. From the Left Gung Jeen Bo perform a Level Cheung technique.

61. While still in the Left Gung Jeen Bo perform a Right hand only Level Cheung maneuver.

62. Slowly lower the tip of your spear toward the floor until it touches.

63. Using a quick snap of the wrist pop the spear upwards and toward you catching it with your right hand near the tassel.

64. Swing the spear forward vertically three times with your right hand.

65. At the end of your third rotation bring the spear behind your back and over your left shoulder while hopping into a Left Diu Ma position.

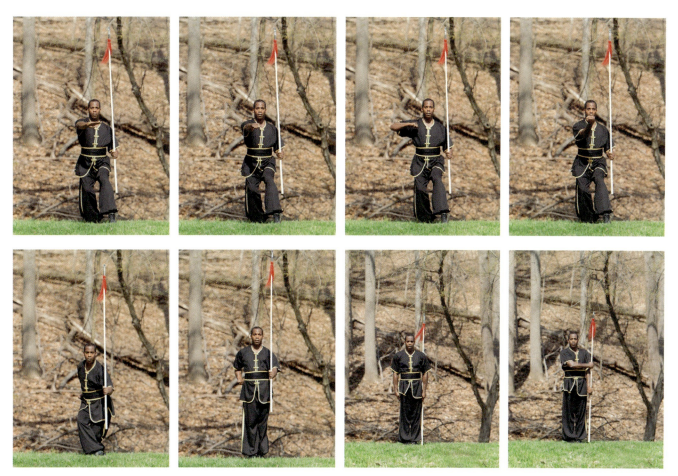

66. Perform movements 5 through 9 again.

67. Stand in the ready position with the spear at your side and the form is complete.

APPLICATIONS
FIRST TECHNIQUE

1. Face each other in the On Guard position.

2. Your opponent attacks with a Level Cheung Strike toward the chest.

3. Step to your right at an angle of 45 degrees into a Sei Ping Ma position and parry your opponent's spear downward using the Kum blocking technique.

4. Counter attack with a Level Cheung to your opponent's chest.

SECOND TECHNIQUE

1. Face each other in the On Guard position.

2. Step forward into a Left Gung Jeen Bo Stance and attack using the Sot technique.

3. Your opponent will then stop your attack with an Over Head Block.

4. Quickly jump turning to your right and dropping into a Right Lok Quie Ma Stance attacking your adversary to the throat using the Sau How Cheung.

A

B

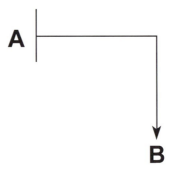

C

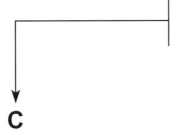

D

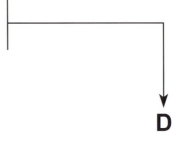

THIRD TECHNIQUE

1. Start from the On Guard position.

2. Pull back into a Right Diu Ma Stance and block your opponent's thrust using the butt end of the spear.

3. Circle parry your opponent's spear while stepping forward into a Left Nau Ma Stance.

4. Continue circling your opponent's weapon outward moving into a Right Gung Jeen Bo Stance attacking with a Jabbing Cheung toward the head of your adversary.

Fourth Technique

1. Face each other in the On Guard position.

2. Your opponent attacks with a Cheung thrust to the chest.

3. Move into a Right Diu Ma at 45 degrees blocking your opponent's attack by using the Kum Cheung technique.

4. Twist into a Right Nau Ma Stance and strike with the butt end of the spear.

5. Step forward into a Left Gung Jeen Bo finishing with a Sot Cheung to the head of your opponent.

Chapter Seven:
Jow Ga Sets from the Dean Chin Branch

7

The Jow Ga system contains over 100 different sets ranging from Empty Hand, Weapon, and various Combat sets. Depending on which branch of the Jow Ga style a practitioner may come from will determine how many and which forms that person may or may not know. For example, the Lohan Kuen set was created by Jow Biu himself shortly after moving to Hong Kong from mainland China (Hong Kong was a British Colony at the time of Jow Biu's arrival). This particular set for the most part looks nothing like many of the other forms taught within the system as it uses a particular type of Pow Choi (Upper Cut Punch) more commonly seen in styles such as Lama Pai or Hop Ga (Knights Clan).

I myself had only just learned this particular form back in 2006 from my training brother, Sifu Rahim Muhammad who is head of the Hung Tao Choy Mei Leadership Institute. He had learned the set on one of his many visits to China gathering information on the Jow Ga system. As a student of the Dean Chin branch of Jow Ga, I along with many of my fellow classmates and instructors have learned the complete version of the Jow Ga system as Master Dean Chin had taught it to us.

One of the things unique to our branch is the various non-Jow Ga sets Dean Chin taught to his students. This is due to the fact that Master Chin had studied other systems of kung fu either before or after completing his studies of the Jow Ga system under his own teacher Grand Master Chan Man Cheung. By doing this, Master Chin gave his students insight into other styles of Chinese martial arts as each style of kung fu has its own unique merits.

The list on the following page are the forms that were taught in the school of Master Dean Chin at the time of his passing in August 1985.

Beginner Level

Stepping Form
Punching Form

Cantonese Phonetic Term	English Translation
Siu Fok Fu Keun	Small Subduing Tiger Fist
Gung Lik Keun	Power Work Fist (Jing Woo Form)
Cern Tao Gwan	Double Headed Staff
Chart Siu Fok Fu Keun	Small Tiger Combat Form

Intermediate Level

Cantonese Phonetic Term	English Translation
Fa Keun	Flower Fist
Chart Cern Tao Gwan	Staff versus Staff Combat Form
Moi Fa Cheung	Plum Blossom Spear
Dai Fok Fu Keun	Big Subduing Tiger Fist
Fu Mei Darn Do	Tiger Tail Single Knife
Darn Do Chart Cheung	Single Knife versus Spear

Advanced Level

Cantonese Phonetic Term	English Translation
Siu Hung Keun	Small Hero Fist
Sup Jee Moi Fa Cern Do	10 Shape Plum Blossom Double Knives
Tit Jeen Keun	Iron Arrow Fist (Village Hung Keun)
Cern Do Chart Cheung	Double Knives versus Spear Combat Form
Fu Hok Cern Ying Keun	Tiger Crane Double Pattern Fist (Hung Ga)
Bao Jong Do	Folding Elbow Knives
Jeet Keun	Intercepting Fist (Jing Woo)
Man Jeet Keun	10,000 Shape Fist

Instructor Level

Cantonese Phonetic Term	English Translation
Jeuk Mei Gim	Swallow Tail Sword (Created by Dean Chin)
Moi Fa Cern Pei Sau	Plum Blossom Double Daggers
Fu Pow Keun	Tiger Cougar Fist
Kwan Gung Dai Do	General Kwan's Big Knife
Chai Jong Keun	Fire Wood Post Fist
Sup Jee Moi Fa Cern Bin	10 Shape Plum Blossom Double Whips
Gwak Jeet Keun	Square Fist
Bat Gwa Gwan	8 Triagram Pole
Gao Wun Dai Do	9 Rings Big Knife
Sam Jeet Gwan	3 Sectional Staff
Bung Bo	Crushing Step (Praying Mantis)
Sam Jeet Gwan Chart Cheung	3 Sectional Staff versus Spear
Gao Bo Toi	9 Step Push (White Eyebrow)
Kwan Do Chart Cheung	Kwan's Knife versus Spear

Now, you may wonder why Dean Chin would teach his students forms from other styles of kung fu when the Jow Ga system was already comprised of concepts from three different styles. Well, lets look at a couple of sets to see what they may offer in the way of training to enhance not only the skill of the Jow Ga student but anyone looking to better themselves as a martial artist.

The form Fu Hok Cern Ying Keun (Tiger Crane Double Pattern) is probably the most famous form in all of Southern China as it was created by the famous Hung Ga Grand Master Wong Fei Hung. As Jow Lung, the main founder of the Jow Ga system, along with his four brothers were first students of the Hung Ga system it would only stand to reason that he would teach this particular form as it represents both the Yang and Yin sides of Southern Chinese boxing.

The Yang or hard side of the form is represented by the Tiger with its brute strength and sheer power in both action and intent. Many of the clawing, punching, and palming actions are accompanied by vocal sounds. The heavy, forceful breathing and strong rooted stances are designed to help generate power in your strikes. The Yin or soft side of the form is represented by the Crane with its light, elusive movements. Yet, it utilizes pin point strikes to vital areas of the opponent such as the eyes, groin, and temple. Grace and poise are the hallmark traits of the employing effective Crane techniques.

The Bak Mei (White Eyebrow) form known as Gao Bo Toi (9 Step Push) was also taught within Master Chin's school. However, not all of Master Chin's students received this particular set. This set was no doubt taught to Dean Chin by one of his uncles. This uncle was an exponent of the Bak Mei system and had taught the young Dean Chin this set in addition to many others within the style.

I myself was one of few students within the Dean Chin lineage to have been fortunate enough to learn this particular set. It was taught to me by my Si Hing (Older Brother) Sifu Raymond Wong who is the founder of the Wong Chinese Boxing Association and an in-door disciple of Master Chin.

Although I do not practice this particular set any longer, I still retain two of the many attributes of the Nine Step Push set which I have incorporated into my Jow Ga training.

The first attribute is speed. Bak Mei is well known for the speed in which their forms and fighting techniques are performed. If you ever get a chance to view a form from this system, all I can say to you is do not blink your eyes. You may miss the whole set. Most of the empty hand sets, when performed properly, normally take about 30 to 35 seconds. The second attribute is aggressiveness. Bak Mei system is an attack oriented type of style. When a practitioner of this style sees an opening or a weakness in their opponent's defense, he goes all in for the sole purpose of taking out his adversary.

Other sets such as Gung Lik Kuen (Power Work Fist) and Jeet Kune (Intercepting Fist) are famous Northern sets most often practiced within the Jing Woo Association. These were founded by the famous Master Huo Yuan Jia who was actually portrayed by Jet Li in the movie *Fearless*. These sets teach more relaxed power and help the Jow Ga student become more fluid in the execution of their movements.

So, as you can see, Dean Chin was in many ways a man ahead of his time. He encouraged his students to not only learn about other styles of kung fu, but to try and gain first hand knowledge of these systems. He encouraged students to study, if not an entire style, at least a part of them. Sifu Chin believed that this expanded the student's overall knowledge of Chinese martial arts.

Chapter Eight: With Respect and Reverence

8

You know, I've been involved in the martial arts for over 30 years. First as a competitor in the open tournament circuit when any and all styles competed against each other in forms, weapons, and fighting. Then, as the Chinese tournament circuit began to take shape, I was able to do pretty good for myself. During this period, I won three east coast and two national titles. Later in 2003, I had the great fortune of winning Competitor of the Year. And on a trip to China in 2004 as a member of the U.S. Traditional Wu Shu team, I was able to win double gold at the first World Traditional Wu Shu Championship held in Zhen Zhou, China. My second trip in the summer 2009 was equally fortuitous as I won Gold and Bronze at the World Guoshu Competition.

However, despite my level of dedication, I and many others who are not of Asian decent would very often hear words of this nature spoken to us, "You can never be good in the Chinese martial arts because you are not Chinese." Now to be fair, there were some teachers like my own Master Dean Chin who would tell us many times, "You can be as good if not better than your Asian counter parts. All you have to do is train." But this, I believe, was the exception to the rule as many Asians along with many Non-Asians felt that Blacks, Caucasians, Hispanics as well as other Non-Asians could never be as good as the people who created and developed this magnificent art form.

I can remember during the late 70's all the way through the 80's between the ages of 12 and 18 trying to see every kung fu movie I could. My friends and I would go see a movie and as soon as the movie let out we were in the middle of the side walk fighting each other trying to mimic the techniques we saw performed on screen. One person would try and imitate tiger claw maneuvers while someone else would try and perform snake techniques. And with all of our boyish enthusiasm to be great warriors we of course shared sentiment that no street fight would be complete without an imitation Mantis stylist and must be included to round things out.

There we were, little martial artist wanna-bes on the sidewalk in front of the Old Town Theater or the Ontario Theater. And of course we all agreed that we had to fight on the concord of the American Theater located at LeFant Plaza South West, D.C. This is what it meant for us non-Asians to be in love with kung fu back in the 70's and 80's. This is how it was for many of us who came up in this time period. A lot of us back then were so in to what we were learning that we became and still are extremely loyal to our masters. Passionate about our practice, we were willing to go great lengths in the pursuit of mastering our chosen art. If you think I exaggerate, then let me tell you two very powerful yet very true stories to show you just how dedicated we as non-Asians were in our quest to become all that we set out to be as martial artists.

During the time of Dean Chin's life, he taught many martial artists who went on to become famous in their own right. Men like Raymond Wong, founder of the Wong Chinese Boxing Association, Hon Lee, co-founder of the Jow Ga Shaolin Institute, Randy Benette who took his knowledge of Jow Ga kung fu to Sydney, Australia, and many others. But none of these men ever did what only one person has ever done in the history of Jow Ga kung fu in America; his name is Craig Lee.

If you came up in Master Chin's school at that time, the name Craig Lee was one that you could not help but hear over and over again. As much as I have won representing this style of kung fu, I can honestly say that Craig marched to the beat of a totally different drum. His career in martial arts began at the age of 12 when his parents enrolled him in the school of Sifu Chin.

Now, in those days classes were two hours long. If Sifu Chin was teaching, it could be three hours in length. That's just how it was back then. With a class lasting up to three hours, you would think that would be enough training time for anybody, but not Craig. There were many times Craig would be in the classroom by himself training for an additional two to three hours working on one technique after another until he got it right.

His dedication to Sifu Chin and the school was so strong that he, without even trying, set a record in the school which stands to this day. As I said earlier, when Craig first joined the school he was 12 years old and practiced harder than any other student at that time. So much so that he trained in the school of Dean Chin seven days a week for not one, but two complete years before he missed his first class.

Oh, did I mention that Craig is Afro-American? Craig's last name just happens to sound as if he was of Chinese decent, but he is very much black. His dedication to training was so strong that he was given the nickname "Young Master" by the senior instructors of the school. This is what I mean by the love that many Non-Asian kung fu stylists like Craig have for the art. Now as far as the record Craig set, it could have been broken in someone else's school, but as far as the school of Master Dean Chin, that record still stands to this day.

Now, if you thought that was something, let me tell you of this next legend of Chinese martial arts. If you lived on the East Coast of the United States on what is referred to as the Mid Atlantic region, the name of the late Josephus Colvin needs no introduction. Kung Fu Joe as he was called by many who knew him was as I said a legend in the game. His career in martial arts began not in the art of kung fu, but in Bando the fighting art of Burma. Sifu Colvin was one of the first people to study the art long before it became popular in the late 80's and early 90's. While still in his late teens, Joe began to take an interest in the Chinese martial arts and became a student of the late Dean Chin sometime between 1968 and 1969.

Sifu Colvin trained hard earning quite a reputation for himself along the way and his thirst for kung fu knowledge didn't end with Sifu Chin. Joe was without a doubt a fanatic when it came to the study of kung fu. So much so, that in the early 70's while still training at Sifu Chin's school during the week, Joe would drive up to New York on the weekends and would train in the Hung Ga system under Master Wan Ching Ming. He did this non stop for a period of about six years!

While Hung Ga was the system that Sifu Colvin promoted, Joe had learned more kung fu than anyone could shake a stick at. Some of the systems he studied include Jow Ga, Chut Sing Tong Long (7 Star Praying Mantis), Ying Jow Pai (Eagle Claw) and Bak Sil Lum (Northern Shaolin) and Nan Tong Long Pai (Southern Praying Mantis system) - just to name a few.

These two individuals and others like them such as myself, have always, since the day we first walked into our Master's school, have and will continue to have a deep love and respect for the Chinese martial arts and the Chinese culture. Many of us back in the old days actually took the time to learn not only the combat, but the language as well with many Non-Asian teachers learning to speak either Cantonese or Mandarin.

Let me tell you of an incident that was told to me by two very well known Non-Asian teachers. This encounter was definitely a lesson for one Asian teacher on how a book should not be judged by its cover. I was in New York's China Town section of the city getting ready to compete in the fifth Annual Summer Bash Chinese Martial Arts Championship hosted by Hung Ga Master and writer Arnoldo Ty Nunez when I had an interesting conversation with two of the late Lama Pai and Choy Li Fut Master Chan Tai San's senior students David Ross and Steven Ventura about a teacher who came to visit them in New York. Before I continue, let me first say that anyone who knows Sifu Ross or Sifu Ventura knows that they speak Cantonese quite well, so to pull the wool over their eyes is nothing short of difficult. They began by telling me of a particular West Coast teacher who came to do a series of work shops and that while in New York this teacher would pay their respects to Chan Tai San. So like any good host, they took this visiting Sifu out for dinner. They then told me that as this teacher and Master Chan began to talk about martial business, the visiting Master began to brag to Chan Tai San about how they conduct classes in their school.

They told Master Chan in Cantonese that they only teach the real kung fu to their Chinese students and to their American students they teach a slightly more watered down version. Master Chan never let on to the visiting teacher that his two students fluently spoke the Cantonese language. So, the old man in effect let this teacher hang them self as his students could understand every word of what was being told to their Master.

Sifu Ross and Sifu Ventura then told me that when they got out of the restaurant they made the following comment to the visiting teacher in the Cantonese dialect letting the teacher know that they understood the complete conversation, "Sifu, we find your method of teaching between Asians and Non-Asians most interesting," They said that they didn't think it was possible for anyone's jaw to hit the ground that fast. I mean just what could this visiting teacher say to them that could possibly defend a comment like that?

The point I want to make is this: what makes anyone of Asian decent think that we as Non-Asians would do anything to misrepresent or dishonor that which we hold most near and dear to our hearts? Many like myself got into the Chinese martial arts in the beginning to learn how to defend ourselves. But, as time went on we discovered that there was far more to learn than just the punching and kicking. We grew to realize that those aspects merely scrape the surface of what martial arts is while people on the outside only see the veneer. Many Non-Asian stylists like Sifu Pedro Ceperro Yee who is of Hispanic decent and an in-door student of Hung Ga Master Frank Yee has learned not only the fighting aspects of his chosen style but also the healing aspects as well having studied traditional Chinese medicine from Master Yee himself.

I mean think about it, do you really think we would put so much of our time and energy into what we were learning for all these years just to treat it like dirt? Many Non-Asians have put in well over 20 years of dedication into the Chinese martial arts through competition, traveling over seas, writing articles for various martial arts magazines, and training of the next generation of kung fu stylist.

Now for me as an Afro-American, I get enough flack just trying to be black in a country that on many levels still treats many minorities like it's the 1950's. Then, I have to deal with it again when it comes to my practice of the martial arts. I can tell you without a shadow of a doubt there are men/women of Non-Asian decent that are more dedicated to the promotion, practice, and development of the Chinese martial arts than some Asians claim to be. On my most recent trip to China in 2009 I had a chance to meet with the sons of the late Jow Ga Grand Master Ho Luk Man who conduct classes at the late Jow Biu's school in Kennedy Town, Hong Kong. When I told them that I was doing a book on the system they said, thank you for caring so much about the system and to please send them a copy of the book when it's completed. After this exchange I wondered if the feeling that some Asian Masters have about Non-Asians not being as good is only here in America because, I didn't see it at all in Asia.

So in conclusion I will end with what I said in my last book, we have to work together in order to reach that common goal that we all want. That goal is for the Chinese martial arts to become accepted and more respected world wide. However, to do this we must work together and be more open minded and accepting of one another and recognize that we do have the same goal. Masters of Asian heritage want their culture to be treated with respect and reverence just as we who are of Non-Asian heritage want as well.

Chapter Nine:
From Kwoon to Stage

On an April evening in 2002, I received a phone call from Chen Tai Chi stylist Stephan Berwick who is a top student of Master Ren Guang Ye. He asked me if I would be interested in traveling across the country on tour doing stage combat with other well known East coast kung fu stylists. I would be traveling throughout the country for a period of three to four months performing in fifteen states within the United States. The only down side for me is that I wouldn't be able to spend time with my two children on a regular basis for a while as I would be on the road rehearsing and then touring.

Unbeknown to me, Stephan had been involved with the creation of an Off Broadway show based in New York featuring Chinese martial arts called "*Voice of the Dragon*" with his kung fu brother and former USAWKF Internal National Champion Jose Figueroa. Also along side Stephan as co-creator of the show would be Fred Ho, founder of Big Red Media.

V.O.T.D., as we called it, was created some time during the mid 1990's and had been seen in smaller venues within New York City. As well, it had been on a smaller tour about two years before I got picked up to perform on what was to be a major tour for this ground breaking show featuring Chinese martial arts. On a side note, if you think the show called *Ra* which was produced by Circus De Soleil was the first big time stage show to feature Chinese martial arts, let me tell you now that they came after us not the other way around. At the end of my conversation with Stephan, he told me to expect a call from Jose within ten minutes with more details about the show and where I would have to go in New York for my audition.

About mid-May of 2002, I took a bus to New York for my audition which was to be at the Brooklyn Academy of Music (BAM). As I got off the elevator, I passed a guy who caught my attention and I thought to myself "He looks familiar," I was right. Before I started my audition, I asked Jose if the guy I passed on the way in was who I thought he was and he told me that it was.

Now, I know your thinking to yourself "Who was it?" Well the guy I passed on the way in was the one and only Bruce Leroy. That's right, the star of the movie "The Last Dragon." Taimak himself was auditioning for the same role that I was there for, but he wasn't ready to demonstrate that day. So, Fred and our director Mira Kingsley were going to have him come in another day.

I said to myself "You have to be kidding" I have to go up against Taimak? A guy who's done film, videos with stars the like Janet Jackson, and god knows who else. This is not going to be my day. My mood walking into the audition wasn't great to begin with as my bus that should have pulled into the city at 4:00 P.M., did not arrive until 7:00 P.M. because all traffic take was detoured into New York as a result of the Twin Towers destruction on 9/11.

My audition consisted of me performing the Jow Ga Bat Gwa Gwan (8 Triagram Pole) and various jumping and spinning kicks along with some of the choreography that was to be in the show. Once my audition was over, I stepped out for a bite to eat with Jose's companion, Natasha, who asked me, "Do you think you have the part?" I told her I didn't think so but that it was cool. I mean come on, I was going to go up against the Last Dragon. What chance did I have?

After about 15 minutes or so Natasha and I walked back to the theater to find Jose, Fred, and Mira on their way out. As Jose handed me my gear that I had left inside, Fred handed me my contract and told me I had until June to get that back to him and that a sort of meet and greet would take place about a month before rehearsals were to begin in mid-October of that year.

As Jose and I took the train back to his place in the North Bronx, he told me that in all the years he's known and worked with Fred on various projects, that was the first time he had ever given anyone their contract on the day of their audition. The next day Jose and I went to a park not far from his place where he began teaching me some of the choreography from the show which would require me to learn new skills and get accustomed to performing techniques for the stage and not for the ring.

Over the next few months, I trained intensely as I was told that our rehearsals would be four days a week and four hours long. Just before I left, however, part of me was extremely worried that I may not get to perform in this ground breaking theatrical piece. You see, the summer of 2002 in Washington, D.C. was in the hands of two men that would soon be known to the rest of the country as the Beltway Sniper.

Near the end of the summer and early fall of 2002, the Washington Metro area was in the hands of John Allen Muhammad and Leroy Malvoe or as the rest of the Washington Metro area would come to know them as the Beltway Sniper. These two men were responsible for the random killings of over a dozen men, women, and children in and around the metro area. No one was safe as the only description anyone had of them was that they drove a white van.

Washington, D.C. is like most other major metropolitan cities. Do you know how many white vans we have in this town? I mean delivery trucks of all kinds, not to mention families who own mini vans. You can't walk two feet without seeing one somewhere in this town. But, this is what we had to deal with until they were finally caught. No one knew who would be next on their hit list or if they would ever be caught and brought to justice. So, it was with great relief that in October I moved to the big apple, New York City, to begin working on what would be the adventure of a life time.

After I got settled into my new home in the North Bronx, I got a chance to meet up with the rest of the cast who would become my new family. The cast consisted of twelve martial artists, six musicians, and a narrator. Performing with me was Chen Tai Chi stylist, Jose Figueroa, Northern Shaolin stylists Gregg Zilb, Philip Silvera, and Earl Weathers, Wu Shu stylist and former competitor of the year, Scott Parker, George Crayton the 3rd son the famous East Coast Grand Master George Clayton Jr. Former gymnast and Wing Chun practitioner, Soomi Kim, model and Hapkido stylist, Lisa Limb, Capoeira and Kali stylist, Sekou Williams, model and Wu Shu stylist, Bilqis Benu, Hung Ga stylist, Kathleen Cruz, and Northern Long Fist practitioner, Jose Quinones.

These twelve people along with our narrator, Jim Yue, and six musicians would be and become my family for the next six months. Let me say I couldn't have asked for a better extended family. With the exception of myself, the rest of the cast was from or had lived in New York for the better part of their lives.

Our rehearsals were four hours long and they were no joke. After we warmed up, which ran about 10 minutes or so, we began to work on the show piece by piece and scene by scene. The show would run 70 minutes in length and was set to live jazz music. Every scene had a different musical score and was to be done in time with the music. So, keeping in time with the band was critical.

Learning new skills such as Northern staff techniques, Chen Tai Chi Broad Sword and modern Wu Shu was exciting as it gave me a chance to not only learn, but appreciate just how difficult it is to learn these other styles of Chinese martial arts. If not for the tour, I may never have had the opportunity to experience these different styles. I think that having done some Northern early on in my training was a big help in learning these new skills because as anyone can tell you, going from one style to another can be difficult sometimes as each system has their own unique attributes.

Anyone in the martial arts who knows me knows that I take my fitness level very seriously as I normally train four to five and sometimes six days a week. But, that first rehearsal put an absolute hurting on me. So much so that when Jose and I got back to his place, I laid on my bed for what seemed to be about ten minutes. In reality I had fallen off to sleep and when I woke up I was still in my clothes and it was 9 A.M. the next day.

After being so worn out from that first rehearsal, I took it upon myself to improve my level of fitness from what it was. You have to understand we were going to be performing in 16 states, 31 cities and 43 shows for a period of 3 months traveling from the West Coast to the East Coast and the Mid West.

The show itself takes a toll on the body as we had to run on and off stage quickly, work with various weapons, an perform group ensemble routines. A well, we had to perform group and individual fight scenes. One of my fights had me taking a jumping back kick square in the chest. Another had me getting clawed in the groin or as we nicknamed it, "*The Castration Scene*" which always and I do mean *Always* got a rise out of the audience and made every man in the theater wince.

With rehearsals over and done, the V.O.T.D. tour left from New York's Kennedy Airport on February the 7th, 2003. Our first stop was Newport, Oregon and all I can say is "Man we had Fun!" I was given the chance to do what many martial artists only wish they could do. This tour opened my eyes and showed me a side of the martial arts that I thought I would never get to experience. If you're a true fan of martial arts movies, then you can't say you have never thought of maybe becoming the next Bruce Lee or Jet Li. So, being picked to perform on stage in front of hundreds of people all over the country was not only an honor, it was also a thrill.

After we landed in Oregon, which was actually the home of one of our cast members, Soomi Kim, I got this crazy idea to make a bet with the entire cast. I bet them that I would be the only member to come off the tour injury free and perform in every show. They told me right then and there that I would get jacked up for saying such a thing seeing how physical the show was and just how many shows we had to do. Never the less I made the bet at which point the entire cast said to me – Your On!

Our bus driver, who was responsible for taking us state to state, was named Bruce Spears. We all thought his was the perfect name for a guy hired to drive around a bunch of martial artists. Newport, Portland, and Eugene, Oregon were the first three stops on our tour. After those shows were completed, we crossed Mount Shasta and headed into California at which point many of us decided to call back home and check on our families to see if all was well and to our surprise it wasn't.

A massive blizzard had struck the entire East Coast from the New England area to the Mid Atlantic region. Depending on where you lived on the East Coast, you could have had anywhere between three to five feet of snow all around you. My mother, who was still living at that time, told me that there was almost four feet of snow all around her and that she was not able to get out at all. However, she was in good shape with plenty of food and water with all power lines in our neighborhood still up and running.

Talk about crazy, here we were traveling, getting paid a good sum of money to perform martial arts across the country and being treated like rock stars while most of our family and friends were busy digging themselves out of one of the worst snow storms the east had ever seen.

As we continued to tour through California, we stopped in Malibu where we had two shows at Pepper Dine University. When we walked onto the campus grounds, we all thought to ourselves, "How on earth can anyone concentrate on studying anything while surrounded with such beauty?" I mean you could see the Pacific Ocean from your classroom. Once we settled in, the co-creator of the show and leader of the Afro Asian band, Fred Ho, invited me out for a bite to eat.

Fred Ho is a very creative man and also a very big one as he stands 6 feet in height. And I found out that he has strength to match the height as I watched him workout one day. As we sat down and ate our meal, I asked Fred just how my name came up in conversation in regards to the show and the tour.

He told me that he, Jose Figueroa, and Stephan Berwick were having dinner talking about who could replace one of the show's original cast members. According to Fred he told them that he wanted to find someone with a strong track record as a competitor who maybe had won a few championships. He also wanted someone who was a practitioner of Southern Shaolin martial arts and if possible he wanted them to be of African American decent.

At this point Stephan told him he had the perfect person and recommended me to become the newest cast member of V.O.T.D. For me it was the opportunity of a life time as I got to perform for thousands of people all across this great country of ours. I got to meet people and see things that I may never had a chance to experience if I had not been picked to be a part of this wonderful cast and crew that I am proud to call family.

Oh yeah, I almost forgot about the bet. Well let me say it this way. Lisa Limb cracked a tooth. Greg Zilb nearly broke a toe. Both Joses pulled their hamstrings. Bilqis Benu fractured her ankle. Soomi Kim bruised her heel. Phil Silvera fell into an orchestra pit. Scott Parker and George Crayton the 3rd took ill. Earl Weathers almost had his nose broken twice. Sekou Williams injured his back. And Kathleen Cruz broke two bones in her right hand. As for myself, I walked away and completed the tour without a scratch.

Chapter Ten: For My Mom 10

From the time I started my training, I had dreams of going to China, the birth place of my beloved Jow Ga kung fu. I would look at the movie 36 Chambers of Shaolin and have visions of myself learning and practicing at the Shaolin temple and thinking to myself, "I wonder if they accept Afro-Americans as students." At one point after some twenty plus years of training and competing, I began to think that I may never get the opportunity to visit China having missed two other opportunities in 1999 and again in 2001 for the Bi-Annual International Jow Ga Kung Fu Federation tournament.

Then in February 2004, I had read that the United State of America Wu Shu Kung Fu Federation (USAWKF), were going to have team try outs for the 1st International Traditional Wu Shu Festival and Championship to be held in Zhen Zhou, PRC.

I thought to myself this may be my last chance to ever get to the place where it all began. Unfortunately, I had a major set back in trying to make this trip a reality. On March 9th 2004, my mother, Mrs. Dorothy Wheeler, who had been told back in 1997 that she had Leukemia passed away at the age of 79.

My mother who had outlived my father by 22 years was able to see her son win three East Coast Kung Fu titles, two National Kung Fu titles, and become the 2003 Male Kung Fu Competitor of the Year. In addition, she witnessed her son perform stage combat as a member of the martial arts theatrical troop, "Voice of the Dragon" that same year in 2003 and be published in various martial arts magazines, but she would not live long enough to see her youngest son fulfill his life long dream of competing in the birth place of Chinese martial arts.

My mother's passing hit me hard and I became seriously ill mainly due to the amount of stress I was under at that time. However, I needed to make a tough decision on whether I was going to still make an attempt to try out for a spot on the USA national team to compete in this most monumental event which was slated for October of 2004.

So in May I made the decision to try out for a spot on the team figuring that the best way to honor my mom's memory would be to go to China and not just medal in my respective events but to win them out right.
.
I trained four to five days a week for at least three3 hours a day. My training sessions were normally at night after I got home from work starting at about 9:00 p.m. and ending at midnight. This schedule was perfect for me as I normally didn't have to be at my job until later in the day. My training routine consisted of heavy cardio and manual resistance training along with drilling my forms over and over to get the timing I wanted just right.

In July of 2004, the USAWKF held its national championship at Northern Virginia Community College in Fairfax, Virginia. During the event, they would also be holding the last of the team trials to determine which men and women would be chosen to represent the United States in international competition.

As the event in China was only allowing each competitor to compete in just two events, the team trials followed the same format. So, I decided to perform the sets Siu Hung Kuen and the Ba Qua Gwan (Small Hero Fist and 8 Triagram Pole). The time requirement for both empty hands and weapons routines was a 45 second minimum to 1:30 second maximum to which I thought ,"That's not a lot of time." But, I knew I could get it done.

I gave a strong performance in both routines with plenty of time to spare and in the end I along with 55 other men and women made the team that would represent the United States at this history making event which was to take place in just three months.

Now, if you've never been to China let me tell you the trip is quite long where nearly 16 hours of your life will be spent in the air. So be prepared and try to get as much sleep on the flight as possible. But if you are like me, you may have problems sleeping on a plane for long periods of time. So, may I suggest that even though it may cost more, get yourself a first class ticket. Going to China was a dream come true and so sleeping for me was next to impossible.

Upon my arrival in China, I was greeted by a young woman by the name of Lena who was to be the team interpreter. We drove to the Beijing International Hotel where I would catch up with the rest of the team who had arrived in China a few days earlier.

The next day the entire team had breakfast together and did a sort of meet and greet as all of us came from different parts of the country and had never met one another before that morning. When breakfast was over, we gathered our gear to take to the airport for the second leg of our trip to Zhen Zhou; the site of the tournament.

Can you imagine being on a plane for 16 hours, flying half way around the world getting about 7 hours of sleep, then taking another plane for an additional hour long flight? I was truly not happy, but it had to be done. Our arrival in Zhen Zhou made me think of all the films I had ever seen of rural China and I can tell you if you think life is hard in America just go to what many consider to be a third world country and I promise you will never complain about how hard your life is again.

The next day, I picked my team warm up suite which we were to wear during the opening ceremony of the event. The one thing I hated about our uniform was that it was completely white. I mean, who was the person who picked the color white to have us wear at this event? It was also at that time that I was told the day and time of my first event. I was told by one of our team leaders, Kyle Cummings, who was a student of USAWKF President Anthony Goh, that I would be the very first competitor in my age group on the floor on Monday morning 7:00 a.m.

If you've ever competed in a martial arts tournament, you know that being first up is most of the time not a good thing as the judges very seldom remember the first competitor on the floor after seeing 30 to 40 other competitors. However, I had a plan in mind that I knew would give me an advantage and all I needed was the unwitting help of the other competitors in order to make this plan of mine succeed.

On October 18th, 2004 at 7:00A.M., the 1st World Traditional Wu Shu Festival and Championship got underway and was held in two venues Zhen Zhou University and at the University gymnasium. I would be competing in Men's Group C where the competitors range in age from 18 to 39.

As we waited in the warm up area, I began to put my plan that was going to give me the first of my two gold medals into motion. I would simply use the nervousness of the other competitors to my advantage by making them over work themselves and gas out mid-way into their performance.

My division consisted of 35 competitors most of which looked very nervous by being in an event of this caliber. When my name was called, I marched to the edge of the carpeted floor and saluted the judges table and once I stepped onto the floor I put my plan into high gear.

Before the competition began, I kept an eye on the other competitors in my division as they warmed up just prior to us taking the floor. Nearly all of them warmed up too much trying to steady themselves for this event. This in my opinion caused them to use way too much energy and so I figured they would not have enough for their performance once the tournament began.

When I stepped onto the floor I ran through my form with plenty of speed, power and balance to spare. The rhythm I used in performing my form was nearly perfect as I hit every stopping point and key high point just the way I had practiced it over and over again for the last three months leading up to the event.

After I finished my performance, I waited along with the other competitors to find out what my final score would be and if my plan was going to work. Just as in every tournament I had ever been in, they dropped the highest and the lowest scores and I was awarded a final score of 8.5.

I looked into the eyes of the other competitors and knew that my plan was going to work after all. I took a seat on the other side of the ring so I could see each competitor's performance and see for myself what I knew was going to happen.

Of the 34 other competitors in my division, not one came close to catching my score until members of the various provincial teams that where representing the PRC stepped onto the floor. In the end my score was strong enough to put me into the Gold Medal group and give me my first of two gold medals that I would take back home not only for my country, my late Sifu Dean Chin, my family and the Jow Ga system, but for my mother who never got the chance to see her son fulfill his dream of going to China and becoming a gold medalist on the international stage.

I Love You Mom.
Rest in Peace.

Chapter Eleven:
I've Seen It Go Wrong

March of 2013 marked the 36 year point for me being in martial arts. 32 of those years were spent dedicating time to the promotion of the Chinese martial arts and in particular the Jow Ga system founded by the famous fighter Jow Lung and his four brothers.

17 years of my time has been on the tournament floor in both the open circuit and the Chinese tournament circuit. I have also participated in and seen many martial arts demonstrations. I have to say that on occasion, I've seen it go badly. Nothing can take the wind out of your sails more if you are a martial artist than a performance gone wrong.

I mean you get out there, bow to the audience, step back into your ready position to begin your performance and all of the sudden, you "Blow It" right in front of everybody and all you want to do at that point is hide, hide, hide. But, if it's not you who wants to hide from the crowd, then it can be all smiles and laughs depending on the situation and how badly that person may have blown it. Let me share with you just a few incidents I've seen happen over the years that made practitioners want to crawl under a rock and say to themselves, "I wish I could start this day over."

In 1983, I had a good friend of mine compete in a dual match up event with one of Tien Shan Pai Master Dennis Browns top students at that time. The event was hosted by Tae Kwon Do Master Mr. MacDuffy of DC Dragons Do Jang. In this one-on-one competition, both contestants had to perform an empty hand set, a short weapon set, and a long weapon set. My friend, Tony Henry, was a top student of Praying Mantis Master Glenn Tapscott and a seasoned competitor. As the event began they both started off with very good scores in both their empty hand and short weapon routines.

When the final event came up, both Tony and his challenger decided to perform the Spear routine from their respective systems. Tony went first and performed a perfect Mantis Spear set with no flaws at all. Then, his challenger performed his set. As I watched the challenger perform, I thought to myself it was going to be hard to pick a winner as both men had done an excellent job up to this point. Then, I saw one of the funniest things I had ever seen. Unfortunately, it was also a very dangerous situation. As the challenger performed a maneuver that placed the spear behind his back and then thrust it in the air catching it with his right hand, the challenger put too much energy into the technique and the spear was launched into the crowd like a missile.

That spear went flying into the crowd like it was shot out of a cannon. I saw three rows of spectators run for their lives. When I saw this, I ran out of the school and laughed so hard I started crying and couldn't go back into the school until I had caught my composure. Needless to say, my friend Tony won the match up and I am pleased to say no one was hurt as a result of the unexpected spear toss.

Other mishaps can be more bone shattering for what should have been a jaw dropping performance. Now, as I recount this event, I can truly say I hope I never see anything like this again. In the early 80's, I use to attend an event given by Karate Master Dale Tompkins called the Eastern Regional Martial Arts Championship.

This open tournament event would bring out the best Japanese, Korean, and Chinese martial artist from all over the east coast. The competition was some of the best that I had ever seen. But, the unique thing about this event was the night finals, which included a breaking event that was always a high point of the tournament. It was at this point that one of the finalists, a second degree black belt, was going to attempt to break 3 large slabs of ice with one single blow.

With all eyes on him, the black belt began the process of building up his Ki (the Japanese and Korean translation for Chi), but was also building up the crowd. We eagerly anticipated what we all hoped would be a most exciting break. He decided to use a Hammer Fist strike to do the job of breaking the ice. As his breathing intensified, he placed his arm across the ice to measure the exact point of contact. He took four very deep breaths and then with a loud yell, brought his arm down on the three blocks of ice. However, things did not turn out as he had planned. Instead of driving his strike straight down through the ice, he pulled his arm back toward himself. I along with the crowd was shocked to see that instead of breaking the ice, he had in fact scraped off all the skin from his right forearm down to the bone. As I said earlier, I have never seen a breaking demo go more wrong than that one and I hope I never will again.

Things can and do go wrong indeed and especially in the ring. At one tournament I saw two extremely skilled black belts go at it, but I could not have predicted the outcome of this encounter for all the money in the world. As I don't know the names of the two men in this incident, I will just call them Tim and Bob. Now, both of these men were in terrific shape and their kicks were both fast and powerful. Many people forget that back in the late 70's and early 80's, point fighting was pretty much like full contact. I remember sparring bare hand and bare foot for the first three years of my competition career. Even the use of head gear didn't become mandatory in all martial arts events until 1989.

The match was one for the ages in my opinion as Tim and Bob both had very good skill and execution in their technique. They were so evenly matched that it was hard to tell who might win. Then, in the blink of an eye, it happened. Bob threw a high spinning back kick at Tim striking him in the jaw. It was so fast that if you turned your head for a split second, you would have missed it.

Tim hit the deck like a sack of potatoes. This kick was right on target and did the job it was intended to do. But what was even more amazing than that was the fact Tim got up so fast from Bob's kick that it shocked everyone. He got up like nothing had happened to him and I thought, "Man this is one tough guy."

Once he got to his feet, the center judge asked Tim if he was alright and if he wanted to continue with the match. He looked at the judge and told him that he was fine and still wanted to fight. The center judge then asked him to face his opponent and get ready to resume the match and this for Tim is where it went wrong. As soon as Tim turned to face Bob, he fell face first on the floor! That's right you got it, a delayed reaction knock out. I've seen people knocked out and I've even knocked people out, but in all my years of training I've never seen anything like that before or since.

As many times as I've been a witness to it go wrong, I have to say that I've also been a victim of it going badly. Here in Washington, D.C.'s China Town, there are two big celebrations that take place each year. The biggest of course is Chinese New Year and the other is known as 10-10 which is Taiwanese Independence Day. Even though I loved performing on Chinese New Year, the Double 10 celebration was a bit nicer because of the weather at that time of year in D.C. It is still very warm and comfortable; somewhere around 60 to 70 degrees.

It had been a few years since our Master Dean Chin, founder of the Jow Ga system here in America, had passed away. While shocked at the untimely death of Sifu Chin, the school managed to carry on and promote the style he had made famous. It was at this point that one of his most trusted students, Master Raymond Wong, moved on to become the founder of the Wong Chinese Boxing Association in order to continue, promote, and spread the teaching of Dean Chin.

The WCBA, as we called it back in the day, started off teaching just two classes a week in a space at George Washington University, but soon found itself with two schools, nearly 60 to 70 students, and classes running 7 days a week. As the reputation of the school rose, so was the expectation of our demos. It was at this point that my gone wrong moment arrived.

As we were preparing for the 1988 Double 10 celebration, Raymond wanted me to perform a Dai Pa (Tiger Fork) set which he had picked up when he went on a visit back to his native village of Toi San, China a year earlier. The form was one of my favorites to perform and practice since I always wanted to learn this weapon after seeing it in a Shaw Brothers movie back in early 1980's.

The form had a maneuver in which I had to roll the weapon around my neck 3 times which I thought was the most exciting part of the form. I practiced the set to get the timing just the way I wanted it so when it came time for the celebration, I would have it absolutely wired.

A week before the parade, I had instructed one of the students in the school named Marcel to check all the equipment that we would be using in the parade; including all the weapons. After I asked him if he had checked all of the items needed in the parade, I found that the tiger fork that I would be using needed a screw put into the head of it so that the blade wouldn't fall off of the staff when I used it.

He told me that he would use a nail to keep it in place. I knew that a nail might not keep the blade of the weapon in place. So, I said to him, "Make sure that blade stays in place or you will be doing a 100 push ups every day for a month." On the day of the celebration, we couldn't have asked for a better day. It was about 70 degrees on a clear sunny day and I along with everyone else in the school was very excited.

The celebration started off as it normally did. First, there was the parade through the streets of China town followed by all the kung fu schools performing the Lion Dance. Speeches were given by various politicians and dignitaries. Then, more Lion dancing at each of the restaurants and other businesses in China town. Then, it came time for our school to perform various Jow Ga forms and weapon sets in addition to two-man sparring sets.

To finish off our performance, I would be performing the Tiger Fork set that I had been practicing for weeks. After Sifu Wong announced me to the crowd, I grabbed my weapon and stepped out into the middle of the street, bowed to the audience, and stood in the ready position waiting to begin my set. Once Sifu began playing the drum, I jumped right into the form giving it everything I had.

The crowd was cheering and I was getting more into the form with each move as I knew my favorite part of the form was coming up. I swung the Tiger Fork around my neck and began to roll it around my neck and down my arm. On the third roll what I didn't want to happen, happened. As I was finishing out the last of the three rotations, the entire head of the Tiger Fork fell into the street! I mean it happened so fast that I only heard two sounds. The first was the sound of cold hard steel hitting the ground and the second was the sound of the audience gasping in disbelief at what they just witnessed. All I could do was quickly stand up, bow to the crowd, and walk back over to my Sifu and fellow classmates as they all said, "Damn! That's messed up." Yup. It happened in a flash. I was on top of the world so to speak in one minute and the next I had egg all over my face. But, I did manage to get a little piece of satisfaction out of it when all was said and done; watching Marcel give me 100 push ups every day he walked into the school for the entire month of November.

Chapter Twelve: The Kindness of a Master

There is a saying within Chinese martial arts that describes the relationship between a Master and a student; "If for one day he is your Sifu, forever he is your Sifu." In the fall of 1983, I got a chance to experience this saying first hand when I saw the kindness of my Master Dean Chin.

In the Washington, D.C. section of China Town, there are two celebrations that all kung fu schools look forward to participating in. The first is the most celebrated, that being Chinese New Year which being a lunar holiday can fall anywhere between the months of January and April. The second holiday which is almost as big is what we call the 10-10 holiday.

The 10-10 holiday is actually Taiwan Independence Day, which is celebrated every year on October the 10th, hence the nick name 10-10, the tenth day of the tenth month. One of the beauties of this holiday is that the weather in the nations capitol still very comfortable this time of year, as it is still in the low 60's to mid 70's degrees. So, all the kung fu schools in the area always looked forward to marching in the parade and Lion Dancing through the streets of China Town.

At the time, I was out of Master Chin's school as I had taken an interest in the Hung Ga system and was training under the late Master Josephus Colvin or as he was affectionately known as Kung Fu Joe. However, I still had many friends with whom I kept in close contact at Master Chin's school. So, the day before the celebration, I made what was suppose to be a quick stop at Master Chin's school to find out what time the festivities were going to start. As I walked into the school, I was greeted by the late Stanley Dea who was an Assistant Instructor in the school and his daughter Stephanie who was also a student in the school.

We made small talk about my training with Joe in addition to just random stuff. Then, Stanley asked me if I knew how to sew? I told him I did know how to sew. He then asked me if I would be willing to give them a hand repairing the holes in the body of the two lions they were going to be using in the following day's parade. I told him that I would be willing to give them a hand with the needed repair of the school's lions. I went back into the classroom and began working on the lions. I could tell each of them had been used a great deal and the wear and tear had taken its toll on them. The work was delicate and time consuming so I could only work on one lion at a time.

While I was working on the lions, Sifu Raymond Wong walked in and asked me what I was doing repairing the lions. I told him that I had been asked to help out with the repairs and that I was nearly finished. He then told me that he wanted me to march with them in the parade the next day. I told him that I didn't want to cause any problems for him by marching with them in the celebration, but he insisted that I participate with them in the double ten celebration.

I finished the repairs on the first lion, and informed Stanley that I would be back in the morning before the parade started to finish the repairs on the second lion as I still had to reinforce the straps that were used to connect the head of the lion to the body. So, as promised I got to Master Chin's school around 9:00 a.m. and got right to work on the second lion. As I was putting the finishing touches on the second lion, one of the other instructors under Master Chin walked into the class room and asked, "What are you doing in this school?" I told him that I had been asked to help with the repair of the lion and was also asked to march in the parade.

He then stormed out of the room. At that point I thought, "Let me finish this job and get out of here ASAP." As I was about to leave, Raymond asked me why I hadn't changed in to my uniform. I told him what had transpired and that I didn't want to cause any trouble for him or Sifu Chin. He told me not to leave and be ready to march with the rest of the school. Once Master Chin did the customary offering to the shrine, we headed out into the street to begin the celebration. The day was just what I expected, sunny with a light breeze and not a cloud in the sky. We went from one restaurant to another performing the lion dance for each owner of the restaurant and guests, many of whom had never seen Chinese lion dancing up close and personal.

When the day finished out around 5:00 p.m., we headed back to the school to both rest and continue the celebration. It is at this point that Master Chin gives out red envelopes with money in them to all his students. Now, depending on how long you have been in the school will depend on the amount of money Sifu would give you. I didn't expect anything because at that time I wasn't a paying student. However, it was told to me that I would receive an envelope because of the work I had done with the lions.

Here's were Master Chin's kindness was shown to me in spades. The instructor who had asked me what I was doing there and didn't want me to march in the parade at all thanked me for my help and then gave me my envelope. Again, I didn't think I was going to get an envelope at all, but after I received mine I thought to myself, "You have to be kidding." One of Master Chin's oldest students and a good friend of mine, Howard Davis, asked me how much I got in my envelope. I didn't say a word, I just handed it to him at which point he looked at me and said. "This isn't what I think it is." He opened the envelope himself and there inside was a single quarter.

As he and I stood there looking at it, Raymond happened to walk by and asked me if I had received my envelope. I told him that I had and was getting ready to leave. He asked how much did Sifu give me and all I could say was "Raymond just let me leave. I don't want to cause trouble." He then took the envelope from me, looked at it and stormed off to the office. I then heard a voice telling me to come into the office.

It was Sifu Chin. He said to me, "I heard what you did for the school and how hard you worked to make sure the school did well in the parade today." He then reached into his pocket and gave me $30.00. He then said to me, "Never forget you are still apart of this family and you will always be welcomed at the school." This was Dean Chin. This was the man who is considered "The father of Jow Ga kung fu in America"; a man who was fair-minded and tried to do the right the thing by all those who knew him.

His act of kindness to a person who was, at that time, no longer a student is probably one of the reasons I went back to complete my training in the Jow Ga system. So, when I see and hear other Masters or their students denounce one another when they have falling outs, which happens from time to time, I don't see an example of a true teacher. Sifu Chin demonstrated what it was to be a true teacher. Master Chin showed me through deeds not words that "If for one day you are his student, for the rest of your life you are his student."

About the Author

Ronald Wheeler has been deeply involved in the combative arts of Western boxing, Chinese kick boxing, and Chinese Kung Fu for nearly four decades. His competitive career has yielded him over 200 awards along with the following major championship titles: United States of America Wu Shu Kung Fu Federation (USAWKF) National Champion 1997 and 1999; USAWKF East Coast Champion 1997, 1999, and 2000; United States Chinese Kuoshu Federation (USCKF) Competitor of the Year 2003; First World Traditional Wu Shu Championship Zhen Zhou, PRC US Team Member Double Gold, 2004; World Guo Shu Competition Gold and Bronze Medal 2009. His interest, commitment, and passion for the fighting arts have propelled him to achieve master level as an instructor. His reverence for martial arts has also inspired him to author the first book written outside of China focused on the martial arts system that he practices; Jow Ga. The title of his first book is, "*The Power of Shaolin Kung Fu*" published by Tuttle publishing 2012. These achievements in turn have been the catalyst for Sifu Wheeler being the first martial arts master within a U.S. major university (George Washington University) to teach a credited course on the Jow Ga system.

Glossary

Cantonese Phonetic Term	English Translation
Biu Jee	Thrusting Fingers
Biu Jong	Horizontal Forearm Strike
Cern Kwa Choi	Double Back Fist
Chi Gung	Practitioner of Developing Vital Force
Chi	Vital Force
Diu Ma	Hanging Leg Stance
Fu Jow	Tiger Claw
Gung Jeen Bo	Forward Stance
Hark Fu Jow	Black Tiger Claw
Hok Yik	Crane Wing
Hung Ga	System of the Hung Family
Choy Ga	System of the Choy Family
Bak Sil Lum	Northern Shaolin
Jit Fu Choi	Tiger Intercepting Fist
Jong Choi	Short Upper Cut
Kup Choi	Diagonal Punch
Kwa Choi	Back Fist
Nau Ma	Cross Stance Moving Forward
Ping Choi	Level Punch
Pow Choi	Upper Cut Punch
Sei Ping Ma	Four Part Horse
Sow Choi	Round Punch
Tau Ma	Cross Stance Moving Backwards
Woo Dip Sao	Butterfly Hands

Ron's Martial Fitness
www.ronsmartialfitness.com

Printed in Poland
by Amazon Fulfillment
Poland Sp. z o.o., Wrocław

70601981R00100